teach us to live

stories from Hiroshima and Nagasaki

Intentional Productions
Pasadena, California 2007

teach us to live

stories from Hiroshima and Nagasaki

Diana Wickes Roose

Book and cover design by Anne Richardson-Daniel
Cover photos from the U.S. Military, 1945. Front cover, Hiroshima. Back cover, Nagasaki.
All photos inside not otherwise credited are from the U.S. Military, 1945, or are courtesy of the individual pictured.

Library of Congress Cataloging-in-Publication Data

Roose, Diana Wickes, 1948-
Teach us to live : stories from Hiroshima and Nagasaki / Diana Wickes Roose.
   p. cm.
 Summary: "Eleven Hibakusha - survivors of August 1945 atomic bombing of Hiroshima and Nagasaki - relate their first-hand experience of the blast and its impact on their lives. Each pleads for abolishing nuclear weapons and promoting peace. Includes original art and poetry, CD of survivors' stories, background on WWII, resources for further information and study guide for educators"--Provided by publisher.
 ISBN-13: 978-0-9648042-8-9 (paperback : alk. paper)
 1. World War, 1939-1945--Japan--Hiroshima-shi. 2. Hiroshima-shi (Japan)--History--Bombardment, 1945. 3. World War, 1939-1945--Japan--Nagasaki-shi. 4. Nagasaki-shi (Japan)--History--Bombardment, 1945. 5. World War, 1939-1945--Personal narratives, Japanese. 6. Atomic bomb victims--Japan--Interviews. I. Title. D767.25.H6R66 2007
 940.54'25219540922--dc22
 [B]

2007031045

ISBN 978-09648042-8-9
© Diana Wickes Roose 2007

Intentional Productions
PO Box 94814, Pasadena, CA 91109
. . . *publishing stories of courage . . .*
human responses to adversity and evil.

To the survivors of
Hiroshima and Nagasaki.
You have given us a great gift. May the
souls of the dead rest in peace.

table of contents

Introduction

The citizens of Hiroshima and Nagasaki witnessed the beginning of the nuclear age. The bombings of Hiroshima and Nagasaki were pivotal events in World War II and the twentieth century, but also in world history. Never before have human beings realized the power to annihilate human society.

The stories told by the survivors of Hiroshima and Nagasaki teach us about the resilience of the human spirit in the face of the horror of nuclear war. Those who survived the two atomic bombings in 1945 witnessed the deadliest acts of war in the 20th century. In a flash, hundreds of thousands of men, women, and children were killed. Many more died in the years that followed, victims of diseases brought on by high doses of radiation.

Those who survived the two atomic bombings in 1945 witnessed the deadliest acts of war in the 20th century.

11

The remains of the Shima
Surgical Hospital,
Hiroshima,
November, 1945

The survivors of Hiroshima and Nagasaki tell us that most victims of war are not soldiers, but children, students, parents, and grandparents. They tell us what could happen if nuclear weapons are ever used again, whether by nations or by terrorists. The survivors know that nuclear weapons should never be used again. No one should have to tell such stories.

The survivors of the atomic bombings tell us that nuclear weapons are truly weapons of terror. Now more than ever, it is important to understand and find alternatives to war. The rise of terrorism has created new dangers, but war as a response to terrorism provides neither safety nor security. War and terrorism make all of us more vulnerable. Both war and terrorism bring with them the possibility of nuclear war, another Hiroshima, another Nagasaki.

Nuclear weapons today are the deadliest weapons of mass destruction, or "WMDs." Trident submarines, for instance, now roam the seas armed with 144 nuclear warheads, each with a force of about 100 kilotons, seven times the power of the bomb with which the U.S. destroyed Hiroshima; some are around 450 kilotons, or 30 times the Hiroshima bomb. More than 27,000 nuclear weapons exist today on earth. Each one could kill more than a million people in an instant. These are not video-game bombs.

To Survive as a Witness

To survive as a witness is an important role in history. Like the survivors of the Nazi holocaust, the survivors of Hiroshima and Nagasaki tell us: never again. Nuclear weapons must never be used again. No one should see what we saw or live so painfully. No more Hiroshimas, no more Nagasakis.

The stories of the survivors of Hiroshima and Nagasaki have faded from memory and are now almost forgotten. The survivors preserve our collective history. We should not hide our eyes and look away – we must recognize the horrors that humans are capable of creating. We must look at these atrocities squarely and learn from them, and then draw our own conclusions.

The survivors help preserve the wisdom of human experience and teach it to our children. What should we learn from them, and how should we live our lives in the light of their witness? This is a question each of us must answer for ourselves. It may mean further study about nuclear weapons and the history and policies that have governed their use. It means facing the responsibilities of being citizens in the 21st century.

For all of us, these stories ultimately raise questions of values as well as politics. The survivors have shown us the importance of forgiveness and

> The survivors help preserve the wisdom of human experience and teach it to our children. What should we learn from them, and how should we live our lives in the light of their witness?

13

teach us to live

To value human
life and dignity is
a responsibility we
must each carry for
ourselves. That is the
real story of Hiroshima
and Nagasaki.

helping others. Acts of compassion are woven throughout their stories and show us how kindness can ease suffering. To value human life and dignity is a responsibility we must each carry for ourselves. That is the real story of Hiroshima and Nagasaki.

Rev. Dr. Martin Luther King Jr. once said that unearned suffering is redemptive. Certainly the survivors have experienced more unearned suffering than most. Their witness begins with acknowledging their deepest feelings. Telling their stories means that they must face themselves and in doing so, find meaning in their lives. Through shared suffering comes wisdom and compassion, and ultimately peace. In telling of their experiences, the survivors of Hiroshima and Nagasaki have become messengers of peace and hope in a nuclear age.

By telling their stories, the survivors of Hiroshima and Nagasaki hope to keep their memories alive even after they die. They show us all the importance of preserving human wisdom and teaching it to our children. The survivors, in this sense, have a very important role to play in the world today. Hopefully this will give some comfort to them as well.

The survivors have picked up the pieces of their lives and found meaningful ways to live, with care and courage. Some became teachers or storytellers, artists or doctors, and many have worked for peace as individuals or with groups of concerned citizens. After all they have been through, they still have hope for the world. Their message can inspire generations to come.

The survivors can also inspire us to make our own choices and teach us about the power of compassion and courage, about the importance of family and faith. Their stories convey wisdom and hope. They can help each of us craft our own unique stories.

"The world grows stronger as each story is told," a Japanese poet once wrote. May the telling of these stories make our world a stronger place.

Our Stories Are All Connected

I was born shortly after World War II ended. I don't remember learning about Hiroshima or Nagasaki in school. My high school history textbook may have had a photo of the mushroom cloud and a few brief sentences noting that two atomic bombs were dropped on Japan, and the war ended.

Today, U.S. history textbooks still typically confine themselves to stating the bare facts, such as this excerpt from one recent American history textbook:

First the United States dropped the atomic bomb on Hiroshima. Two days

"The world grows stronger as each story is told," a Japanese poet once wrote. May the telling of these stories make our world a stronger place.

15

In 1980, I worked as a journalist researching American military and nuclear policies. I was offered a grant from the Hiroshima International Cultural Foundation to travel to Japan to interview some survivors of the atomic bombings.

later, the United States dropped a second atomic bomb on Nagasaki. On August 10 the Japanese government asked for peace.

--Lewis Paul Todd and Merle Curti, Triumph of the American Nation

No hint of controversy, no allusion to the number of deaths or the fierce debates about nuclear weapons that erupted at the time and continue to this day, no invitation to consider the implications of President Truman's decision to drop atomic bombs on the citizens of two large Japanese cities.

I never learned about Hiroshima or Nagasaki until I was an adult. In 1980, I worked as a journalist researching American military and nuclear policies. I was offered a grant from the Hiroshima International Cultural Foundation to travel to Japan to interview some survivors of the atomic bombings. I later produced documentaries about their stories and have returned to Japan several times since then to visit and keep up with their unfolding stories.

On my first long airplane flight to Japan, I began to worry. I might not be alive if not for those atomic bombs! My father had been a soldier in the US Army in the Pacific during World War II, training to invade the Japanese islands. If the war hadn't ended, he might have been killed along with thousands of other Americans and Japanese. He would not have returned home in 1947, and had twin daughters, my sister and me, a year later. Ironically, I owe my life partly to a twist of fate that spared my father but destroyed the lives of hundreds of thousands in Hiroshima and Nagasaki.

Later I asked my father whether he had felt any guilt about the horrific consequences of the atomic bombs. Like most Americans, he thought the bombs had ended the war and saved countless American and Japanese lives. He had never felt guilt, only relief. "Harry Truman saved my life," he said. "We were just happy the war was over."

Nevertheless, I harbored a few feelings of guilt. How would the survivors feel about Americans? Would they hold us responsible for their suffering? And what about the next generation? Do we derive any secondary responsibility for the deeds of our fathers?

When I arrived in Hiroshima, I was surprised. Although the city had been completely destroyed in 1945, I saw modern, bustling streets, office workers hurrying to catch streetcars, beautiful parks with children playing.

But first glances are deceiving. Memorials to the dead are everywhere -- in banks, offices, and department stores, niches on street corners and in parks and schools. The atomic bombings are inextricable parts of the past and present in

How would the survivors feel about Americans? Would they hold us responsible for their suffering? And what about the next generation?

More than 3,000 people died in the terrorist attacks on September 11, 2001. In Hiroshima on August 6, 1945, some 140,000 men, women and children were killed instantly or soon thereafter.

Hiroshima and Nagasaki. The scars and memories are still vivid.

Hiroshima reminds me of New York City after the 9/11 World Trade Center attacks. Both cities have memorials as reminders of the deep scars that remain for those who survived. More than 3,000 people died in the terrorist attacks on September 11, 2001. In Hiroshima on August 6, 1945, some 140,000 men, women and children were killed instantly or soon thereafter.

On the morning of September 11, 2001, I talked with Ms. Etsuko Nagano, a survivor of the atomic bombing of Nagasaki. I had invited this tiny gentle lady to my town in Ohio to speak at an exhibition. Her story is included in this book.

As news of the World Trade Center attacks came on the television, Ms. Nagano was talking with a group of children in the school library. The air was electric with fear and alarm as teachers began crying and parents came to retrieve their children. Ms. Nagano stopped in the middle of her story and said, "I think terrorism is terrible, and I am very sorry. We all hate war."

Like many Americans after 9/11, many survivors of Hiroshima and Nagasaki responded initially to the bombings with hatred and bitterness. Some felt there was no one to help them in their time of darkness. But with the kindness and care of their families, doctors, priests, and counselors, the survivors gained wisdom from their suffering. They now teach us that violence engenders more violence, and war creates hatred and revenge. They believe that only by living peacefully can we find the path to peace.

After 9/11, I began compiling the stories told to me by the survivors of Hiroshima and Nagasaki. Most were translated and edited from my own interviews in Japan. Several were written by the survivors themselves. Some included their art and poetry as well. I am very thankful and humbled by their generosity in helping to bring this collection of their stories to life.

Ms. Tazu Shibama was the first atomic bomb survivor I met in Hiroshima. On the morning of August 6, 1945, she sat in her kitchen eating a simple breakfast. Mr. Sumiteru Taniguchi was riding his bicycle delivering mail on the morning of August 9 in Nagasaki. In a flash, their stories and countless others became important narratives of our history. I hope this collection will help preserve them for our children and generations to come.

Diana Roose

April 2007

After 9/11,
I began compiling
the stories told to
me by the survivors
of Hiroshima and
Nagasaki.

The Postscript to My Letter

Ms. Tazu Shibama, 1980

Dressed in typical Japanese kimono, Tazu Shibama quietly introduced herself in English. She explained that she was educated in the United States in 1930. She had a missionary scholarship and received teacher training at Peabody College in Nashville, Tennessee.

Ms. Shibama was a schoolteacher in Hiroshima. She lost 350 of her students and 18 fellow teachers in the atomic bombing. Her father was too old to help during wartime, so he had gone to live with her older sister in the countryside. She lived by herself in a house about 1.5 kilometers from the center of the explosion.

21

Ms. Shibama taught school for many years. The atomic bombing gave her a mission, her postscript, as she called it, to her life. She felt a responsibility to teach young people about the horrors of nuclear weapons.

After the war, Ms. Shibama left the school and lived by herself in Hiroshima. She never married. Food was very scarce, and life was difficult. She thought her English speaking ability could help other people, so she moved to another city near Hiroshima and started a small private English language school. Without anyone's help, she ran the English Institute herself.

Over the years, many young girls and boys came to her house to learn English. They didn't know much about the atomic bombings that happened before they were born. So every year as August 6, the anniversary of the bombing, approached, Ms. Shibama put aside a special time for them to ask questions and talk about it. The Japanese government had discouraged talking about peace and the atomic bombings immediately after the war, so public schools didn't give this subject much time. Private schools such as Ms. Shibama's had more opportunities to teach young people about these issues.

Ms. Shibama taught school for many years. The atomic bombing gave her a mission, her postscript, as she called it, to her life. She felt a responsibility to teach young people about the horrors of nuclear weapons. Seeing the grass grow again in Hiroshima brought reassurance that she could survive, but her work as a teacher gave her life meaning and hope.

I must say that I am very, very lucky to have survived because that day, August 6, was a Monday and I was just having my simple breakfast in my kitchen. At 8:15 there was a flash. The next moment, all was dark. I was buried under the fallen house.

As I sat in the darkness right after the bombing I thought, here I must die. I thought surely many other people were killed at that time, so it was natural for me to be dead as well. All these years of living are like a postscript to a letter. When you finish your letter and you want to say a little more, then you put P.S. and write more. So my life after the bomb is my P.S., the postscript of my letter.

I sat in the darkness for about 10 minutes, and then I heard somebody moving near me. It was my neighbor. He had been standing in his garden, about 50 yards away. Instantly the blast threw him down and buried him in the same place where I was, under my broken house. He was strong enough to make his way out, and he pulled me out. I was saved before the fire came. Many, many people were not killed instantly, but buried under their houses and burned to death – burned alive.

My neighbor went back to his house. Of course all the houses were burning. He tried to save his wife and two daughters, but he was unable to save any of them.

"Many, many people were not killed instantly, but buried under their houses and burned to death - burned alive."

23

"Hundreds and hundreds of people were exposed to radiation in the streets. They were already burned, their faces with skin hanging, their clothes all gone. Some of them had shoes — only shoes — walking just like ghosts."

He stayed there for about a week. We did not know anything about the poison that spread in the air. My neighbor drank the poisoned water and breathed the poisoned air. He died after two weeks. So all his family was lost.

After the air raid siren, I began to walk to the countryside where my father was staying. I walked all day long because there were no trains or busses, nothing to ride.

I came to a wooden bridge near Hiroshima station. It was burning. I was barefoot and it was so hot. I had to run across the burning bridge. Water was running underneath the bridge, but still the bridge was burning.

Hundreds and hundreds of people were exposed to radiation in the streets. They were already burned, their faces with skin hanging, their clothes all gone. Some of them had shoes -- only shoes -- walking just like ghosts. Their shock was so great, they lost words, they couldn't speak. Even little children did not cry. They just walked quickly to get out of this terrible place.

In the countryside, my sister gave me fresh vegetables to eat, some eggs and other food. After staying in bed for about two weeks, I was strong enough to get up again. I lived there for about ten months. But of course, all of Hiroshima was destroyed.

Seeing Hiroshima today is like a miracle to me, because when I stood in front of that smashed railroad station, all I could see was the hill on the other side. All the houses and factories were gone. I thought it never would be rebuilt, because people said that when the A-bomb destroyed a city then nothing could live or grow for 75 years. But strangely enough, when spring came the next year, flowers started blooming and I saw green grass everywhere. That gave us hope to live.

More than half the population of Japan today was born after World War II, and they don't know anything about war. It's very difficult to know what war means. They don't know what suffering we saw. Some, on the other hand, find it too sad to look at, too extreme. They see pictures with some of the stories they hear, but they cannot correctly judge what to think about war because they don't know anything, after so many years have passed.

The Japanese people, including statesmen as well as civilians, enjoy peace so much. With the improvement of the economy, most people are quite satisfied. They forget the danger of war. They say peace, peace, without sincerity. They avoid thinking about it. But if the nuclear powers continue an arms race, who knows how it will end? Who can tell what will happen in the future? If war starts, in a real sense Japan too will be a miserable victim.

"I don't know about America, but I think many people like to talk about peace, but the majority of them are rather indifferent, don't you think?"

25

"My message is that weapons, no matter how big they are, cannot bring peace to this world."

I don't know about America, but I think many people like to talk about peace, but the majority of them are rather indifferent, don't you think?

Weapons are no good. My message is that weapons, no matter how big they are, cannot bring peace to this world. Only love and friendship can give us a peaceful life, so let's be friends. I will try to do my best. I hope you will do your part. Our responsibility is to teach children, to teach everyone I believe, about the horrors of nuclear weapons. That is my only wish.

Something Felt Funny On My Back

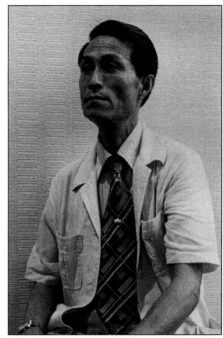

Mr. Sumiteru Taniguchi, 1980

S umiteru Taniguchi was 16 years old when the atomic bomb was dropped on Nagasaki. He was on his bicycle delivering mail in the countryside about two miles from the explosion. As he pedaled, he heard the sound of a plane in the distance. He looked back and saw what looked like a rainbow.

The color photograph on the next page was taken in November of 1945 and shows Mr. Taniguchi several months after the bombing. His back was burned raw, and the radiation made his burns heal improperly. He was hospitalized for more than three years– longer

Sumiteru Taniguchi, age 16, in the hospital

than any other survivor. He has had many operations and skin grafts, and his back is covered with scars.

As a young man, Mr. Taniguchi reacted to the bombing with anger -- at his injuries, at his parents for not warning him about war, and at war itself. Finally his anger was transferred into action. As he thought about the people who had died, while he himself was still alive, he realized that he must live on their behalf. He believes he must tell what happened, so they will not have died in vain.

Despite his poor health Mr. Taniguchi has spent his life telling the world about the dangers of nuclear weapons. He has testified at the United Nations and in many countries. He has been president of the A-Bomb Sufferers Council, chair of the Young People's A-Bomb Association, and a member of the Japanese Council for Prohibition of A & H Bombs. He has dedicated his life to being a witness.

Everything happened in a flash. All I remember is that I was blown about three meters. I hit the ground very hard. I lay there and thought perhaps a big bomb had just exploded nearby. I raised my face and tried to look around.

I saw that all the little children who had been playing near me were blown away and scattered all over, like specks of dust. I thought I would die there. But I scolded myself for my weakness and got up. My bicycle was twisted like soft toffee.

I thought that something felt funny on my back. Something was running. It was slippery all over my back. The skin on my left arm was hanging down from my shoulder.

I immediately felt hatred for war. When I was little we were all told to glorify war. Everything connected with war was splendid. That was drummed into me. But this experience of being hit by a bomb revived all the feelings against war that had been dormant in me. I cursed my parents and members of the older generation for not warning me against war.

I tried to reach an air raid shelter on one of the hills that surround the city of Nagasaki. When I reached the bomb shelter, I collapsed. I couldn't move an inch further.

For about two years, I lay in a sick bed. I couldn't move. I lay face down, motionless. Since my body was full of agony and pain, I cried and shouted at the medical doctors to kill me. Even a few doctors who were treating me gave up their attempts to save my life and were surprised to see me alive every time a new day arrived.

Four years after the bombing, I was in better condition and could move a little bit.

"For about two years, I lay in a sick bed. I couldn't move. I lay face down, motionless. Since my body was full of agony and pain, I cried and shouted at the medical doctors to kill me. Even a few doctors who were treating me gave up their attempts to save my life and were surprised to see me alive every time a new day arrived."

31

"When I started feeling pain, this pain gave me tremendous joy because I knew that I was alive."

The wounds on my back were only half healed when I was discharged from the hospital. But I had a new anxiety. Could I get a job? How would other people look at me? Quite often I cried with fear and anxiety, all by myself.

Finally after many years I recovered from my wounds and regained my health. I decided to have a major operation to remove all the scars on my back and elsewhere. I was afraid my health was not so good because my rotten flesh had been infested with maggots.

Though I was still alive, a couple of times I stopped breathing. I thought death would relieve me from everything. When I started feeling pain, this pain gave me tremendous joy because I knew that I was alive.

My body was badly burned and the scars on my body do not perspire. On a very hot summer's day, since I cannot perspire, it feels like I'm carrying a great burden made of raw cotton.

I noticed that a part of my wound had formed a tumor. The tumor broke and was about to become a cancer. I had an operation and that particular cancer was removed. The wound did not heal. Therefore it was necessary to graft the skin from another part of my body. I have to go to the atomic bomb hospital at least once a month to see if the tumor is behaving all right.

Mr. Sumitern Taniguchi

This has been my life for more than 60 years. All the injuries I sustained are not the only cause of my suffering. Psychologically, mentally, this life of mine has been a life of agony. I have not had much pleasure in living. I have not enjoyed life like every young man or woman is entitled to.

I've hated war ever since I was injured by the bomb. I look at school children and I pray. Seeing children makes me feel that the world should get rid of all nuclear weapons. We must create a freer and more peaceful world.

Summer is a very difficult season for all atomic bomb survivors. But despite the heat, every year I ask all of my friends to work harder and harder for a peaceful world without nuclear weapons. This is my only remaining wish.

We have to make sure that all wars or conflicts disappear from the face of the earth. The nuclear weapons that are stockpiled by nations of the world can kill all mankind, I hear. If something happens, in time mankind will disappear from the earth. Perhaps the planet earth will be destroyed at the same time.

Please tell your friends and people living in your community how horrible a war can be, how horrible the explosion of a single bomb can be, so that they will work harder for peace. Thank you very much.

"Please tell your friends and people living in your community how horrible a war can be, how horrible the explosion of a single bomb can be, so that they will work harder for peace."

33

I Try to Create My Own Peace Movement

Ms. Suzuko Numata, 1990

35

S uzuko Numata lost one leg in the atomic bombing in Hiroshima. I was struck by her friendly and quiet demeanor. As she sat and took a handkerchief from her purse, she reminded me of my grandmother.

Ms. Numata has used her disability as a way to start conversations with strangers about her story and her hopes for peace. She carries postcards and folded paper cranes with her always and gives them to people she meets. She is a one-woman peace movement.

"As I looked back, I saw large flames in the windows as if red curtains were flickering there. If I hadn't been rescued, a little later I would have been burned and died."

Ms. Numata was 21 years old at the time of the bombing. She had been working at the Hiroshima Post & Telecommunications Bureau, about a mile from the explosion. Although the bomb nearly destroyed her life, Ms. Numata overcame her pain and suffering by teaching and learning how to tell her story. The urge to teach others is a powerful healing force.

I was cleaning my office at the top of the building. Some of my co-workers were exercising outside under the blazing sun and clear, cloudless sky. We did not know what was going to happen to Hiroshima, which turned out to be an evil fate.

I finished my cleaning and was going downstairs when I saw a sudden flash in front of me. Its color was like all the colors of the rainbow. I cried out and fainted, and was blown away by the blast.

When I woke up, I found myself under heavy debris in a dark room. I couldn't move, and I repeatedly fainted. I heard someone calling, "Is anyone here?" I cried for help in a loud voice. A man heard me and pulled me out. He carried me on his back because I couldn't walk . My left foot was almost cut off. The corridor was full of smoke, but we managed to go down to the first floor and went out into the yard. As I looked back, I saw large flames in the windows as if red curtains were flickering there. If I hadn't been rescued, a little later I would have been burned and died.

Trees in the yard were burning and many people were seriously injured. As the blaze was reaching us, we tried to move to a safe place. It was then that my father found me. I was laid on a mat for a stretcher and carried away.

It was like hell, fire blazing, smoke here and there, injured people who couldn't be identified as man or woman, crying "water" or "help" and then dying. Suddenly the sky became dark and it started to rain. The rain hit my ankle but I didn't feel pain.

The hospital next door was burned. Doctors and nurses were also injured, and no one had any medical treatment. When night came, we went into the entrance of the building where the flames had died down, for we feared another B-29 attack. The entrance was full of injured people.

The next morning I was transferred to a hospital nearby that became a temporary rescue station. I was there for three days. My leg became gangrenous. On the third day, a doctor examined my leg and told me it would have to be amputated to save my life. So I had an operation on August 10th. My life was saved but the wound didn't heal. I was hospitalized for one and a half years and had four operations.

"It was like hell, fire blazing, smoke here and there, injured people who couldn't be identified as man or woman, crying "water" or "help" and then dying."

37

"In 1946, I met an American who came to Hiroshima as a member of a camera crew from the United States. He wanted to take a photograph of me. This was seven months after the bombing and I was still in great pain."

38

My sister was seriously injured on her face and arms by fragments of glass. My older brother was burned on his face and chest. My mother was caught under the fallen house and injured her arms. My father didn't have any external injuries, and our family was reunited about two weeks later.

On the morning of August 6, I had been very excited to think of August 10, because that was the day when my fiancé who was in the army at the front was going to come back and we were going to have a wedding soon. That morning I was very happy. I had two dreams: after marriage I would become a good wife and a good mother of our children. But later on I found out my fiancé had already died in July, so he wasn't coming back. And on top of that, I lost my leg. I felt I had lost all happiness.

For many years, I always wore a kimono to cover my leg. Most people did not know that I was an atomic bomb survivor. But I always felt I wanted to tell what I saw on that day.

In 1946, I met an American who came to Hiroshima as a member of a camera crew from the United States. He wanted to take a photograph of me. This was seven months after the bombing and I was still in great pain.

We went up to the roof of the building where I had worked. When I was asked to stand in front of a camera I thought nothing of it at first. I remember the *interpreter was kind and asked me softly, "It must be very painful, but would you please take off your bandage?" I did what I was told.*

I had a bandage on my leg, and on top of the bandage was a knitted wool cap. I never forgot the moment he took my picture. I always felt that if I could find that particular picture, it would help me tell my story as a survivor.

Then in 1981, some of the films and photographs taken at that time were brought from the United States and returned to Japan. That's when I found the picture of myself that was taken so many years ago.

When I saw the photograph, I was shocked. What shocked me most was the scene from the top of the building. I could never forget it. Until then, I hadn't seen the whole burnt city. That was very impressive.

When I look at that photograph now, I feel -- I was so very young. When I look at my leg now, it's much thinner and it has all these wrinkles. Then I was very young and had very nice legs.

It was very difficult when I was in my thirties. The city was being rebuilt and people were picking up their lives and going on. I felt left out since I lost my marriage. But what supported and encouraged me was meeting people and becoming friends.

"When I look at that photograph now, I feel — I was so very young."

39

"I'd like you to understand that I had to overcome great feelings of shame as a woman to show a very important part of my body to other people. But in order to work for peace, I had to overcome that feeling."

Later on, some films were made based on those photographs, and I appeared in the first film. When some of my former students saw me in the film, they asked, "Why didn't you tell us about your experiences? You have to teach children about peace and not war." Some of my former students had children and even grandchildren. Their words touched my heart, and I decided that I should start telling my story.

At first I felt very embarrassed to have my leg seen by so many people. I wanted to hide the fact that I was an A-bomb survivor, and that I have only one leg. Those were the things that it was hardest for me to reveal. However, I also felt it was my responsibility to tell my story.

I had to become brave enough to tell my story, especially to young people, because war should never break out again in the future. What I could do, I thought, was to tell what had happened to me.

I'd like you to understand that I had to overcome great feelings of shame as a woman to show a very important part of my body to other people. But in order to work for peace, I had to overcome that feeling. Now I don't feel any shame. By showing these things to others, I can convey what happened in the past for the sake of world peace.

When I thought of the people whose faces were burned by the bomb when they were young, and they didn't dare look at mirrors, I didn't feel good about hiding my leg. If I wanted to, I could hide my leg, even now. But as long as I hid my leg, my thoughts about the atomic bomb wouldn't be conveyed to future generations. So I had to overcome those feelings.

I have a picture of an aogiri [Chinese parasol] tree that was exposed to the atomic bomb at about the same spot where I was exposed. This tree has been transplanted into the peace park in Hiroshima. Whenever I see it, I am encouraged because it has survived and continues to live, just like me.

For many years, I kept my mouth closed. I shut my mouth and shut my mind too. But since I found the aogiri tree, it encouraged me to tell my story. Without that tree, perhaps I wouldn't be telling stories, even now.

I always think about how many children I would have, how old they would be now, and how many grandchildren I would have if there had been no war, no atomic bombing. Those are the thoughts I always have since I lost my fiancé and my leg because of the war. I lost my marriage. I couldn't think about having children or grandchildren at all.

In 1951, I became a teacher. I taught school for 26 years. Sometimes the students came to me for help. Some people have problems in their love

"I always think about how many children I would have, how old they would be now, and how many grandchildren I would have if there had been no war, no atomic bombing."

41

> "After my long period of silence, I felt only the survivors could convey the meaning of Hiroshima to others. When I thought about that, I was encouraged."

relationships or they can't get married for some reason. In the past I arranged marriages for them and helped sort out their problems with their love relationships. Now those students call me not teacher, but grandma. That really makes me happy. I'm very glad I can do something for others.

At first I felt very uncomfortable being called grandma. But ever since I started telling my story, I meet so many children. Especially when I meet very young children I ask, "Do I look like a young woman? Do I look like somebody's mother? " And you know the really little mouths of those young children? They open their mouths wide and say, "No!" Then I ask, "Do I look like a grandma?" Everybody loudly says, "Yes, you do!" That's when I feel happiest. Being called grandma by children is a great blessing, the reason I feel very lively.

I had no idea how to start telling my story to children, how to talk about that day and my life after the war. When I thought of the past and my friends who died, however hard I tried to talk, I could only weep. I couldn't verbalize my feelings at all. I tried to do better, but again I still couldn't do it. Only tears fell from my eyes.

I had to tell them what had happened, so I couldn't very well keep crying. So I became much calmer. After my long period of silence, I felt only the survivors *could convey the meaning of Hiroshima to others. When I thought about that, I was encouraged.*

In order to change people's minds, sometimes things like a photo or a chance meeting can influence someone very much. These influences are very important, I believe. In my own case, I broke my silence because I saw a photograph and people encouraged me. Some writing or a picture can be seen by many people. Eventually I think these things will help people change their minds.

I made postcards of the aogiri tree that survived the bombing, and I folded paper cranes. I always carry these with me. When I meet people, maybe in a restroom when I meet a mother and child, or maybe at the airport or at a restaurant, I hand it to them and try to make a new relationship with them, so that I can convey my feelings to them. I try to create my own peace movement. I believe it's important to start with the people around me.

When I see young people I strongly feel I should not let them go through the same experiences that I did. That's why I tell them to value and nurture themselves and make their youth very important and meaningful. You can never go back to your youth again. I feel a responsibility to help young people have a great future.

被爆した "アオギリ" は生きる
Atomic-bombed "Aogiri" trees in Hiroshima, which have revived from the damage.

"We can hate nuclear weapons, but we shouldn't hate people. If we really want peace, hatred is our enemy."

Last year I met a group of mothers and children and I gave paper cranes to them. I was happy to learn that they already knew what the cranes meant. I was happy to work as an ambassador for peace. Now many people who support this movement help me by folding paper cranes. I'm very grateful.

Of course some students ask me questions. I tell them that right after the war I was angry at the United States. However, living and surviving all these years I overcame those feelings. I realized that as long as we have hatred toward each other, we can't build peace. We can hate nuclear weapons, but we shouldn't hate people. If we really want peace, hatred is our enemy.

I look very healthy now, but I have to wear a corset because my hip bone is distorted. I think it is an aftereffect of the bombing. A few years ago I had an operation again on my leg because I've always had pains in my leg. The doctor was afraid something might be wrong with my leg bone. And then the pain stopped. However, when it gets very cold, it tingles. But since I am so busy telling my stories I've had no time to go to the hospital.

I feel maybe my time is not so very long now. It may only be a short time that I will be able to continue to testify about my experiences. I survived the atomic bomb and have been encouraged by many things including this tree. I'd like to lead a very active and meaningful life. That's why I feel a great urge to tell my story now, not later. I'm determined to work for peace for the rest of my life, having courage and making steady efforts to tell my story. Even at this moment I can't forget that terrible experience. I will never forget.

Child placing paper cranes at the Hiroshima Children's Monument, August 6, 1980

45

We Don't Need Any More Survivors

Sunao Kanazaki lost seven family members in the atomic bombing of Hiroshima. As a witness to history, he has drawn pictures of the tragedy, such as frightening mushroom clouds, black rain, a boy covered with blood, a wailing woman standing in front of a destroyed house, and a mother and a child whose entire bodies are burned. Mr. Kanazaki wandered the city that was turned into a desert by the bomb and sketched his pictures.

Mr. Sunao Kanazaki, 1988

"Suddenly a blinding ray of light split the sky."

48

Mr. Kanazaki's pictures have been vividly resurrected in the form of an animated documentary film entitled "Burned to Heaven." The people in the film look at us without sorrow or anger. How can we respond to these eyes?

I have always liked to paint pictures, ever since I was a boy. Now and then people said my pictures were good, so I thought maybe I'd be a painter. Just after I turned 20, my work was beginning to get some recognition from the art world, so I was assuming I would wind my way toward being an artist. But that bomb changed my life.

In 1945, I was living with my wife and children about 2 kilometers from the place where the bomb exploded. On August 6, I'd gone to work at a military factory about 15 kilometers west of the city.

It was morning and we were just about to start work. Suddenly a blinding ray of light split the sky. Amazed by this eerie light, I bolted out the door. The ray had disappeared but overhead a mushroom-shaped ball of fire was swelling up with tremendous speed, as if swallowing up the blue sky. Then we were attacked by a roar that seemed to burst our ears and a violent blast.

When I came to, I'd been smashed to the ground. All these events happened in a single instant. Brushing off the dirt and debris, I ran up onto the riverbank for a better view. The whole city was engulfed in white and black smoke.

With this terrifying scene before me, the faces of my wife and children trembling with fear floated through my thoughts. An uncontrollable anxiety took over, and I hurried back to the factory office.

The factory windows, even the frames, were all blown away. My co-workers who had been slow getting out were badly cut by the flying fragments. They were bleeding and in pain. I took off for the streetcar stop.

People were running away, carrying what they could in their hands. When I finally threaded my way through the confusion to the streetcar stop, I could see the trains weren't running. I'd have to walk home.

I couldn't help running. Soon I saw a military truck coming out from town. In that instant, my anxiety turned to terror. The truck was packed full of blackened human beings that looked more like charred lumber. What about my wife and children? I fought to banish that thought and kept running.

As I entered the next town, huge drops of black rain began to fall. Electric poles were leaning crazily. Huge trees were toppled. The road was full of signboards and other junk. There was no one in sight. The town was dead.

I took a road through the rice fields. People were scattered along the road, lying in the black rain looking like tattered rags. I couldn't tell if they were dead or alive. I found myself crying as I ran.

I came to Asahi Bridge. My hometown was just on the other side. Crowds of people burned beyond recognition were lying in piles at the foot of the bridge. The railing had been blown away. Lots of boards were missing and flames were licking up all over it. In desperation, I jumped and ducked my way to the other side.

My house was flattened completely. Calling their names over and over, I searched for my wife and children, tossing aside whatever debris came to hand. But I couldn't find them. The riverbank was covered with people so totally transformed that I couldn't tell who was who. Still I went from one to the next, checking. My family wasn't there either so I decided to try the elementary school in the next town.

"People were scattered along the road, lying in the black rain looking like tattered rags. I couldn't tell if they were dead or alive. I found myself crying as I ran."

50

The roadsides were crowded with the ones who had fallen, their arms sticking up in the air, lying in the burnt weeds. The only one still alive was a young girl who turned to me for help. "My parents are waiting for me. Please, won't you take me home?" she asked.

But I couldn't do it. A request from a young girl on the brink of death, and all I could do was walk away. I can still feel the intense guilt and self-loathing of that moment.

Drops of water from a twisted pipe were falling into a little puddle. A group of young girls had been crawling toward it for a drink of water. They never made it. They lay where the last of their strength had left them.

The road to the elementary school was a parade of eerie figures burnt over their entire bodies, skin hanging down in shreds, eyes swollen shut, both arms held weirdly out in front of their chests. They walked along crying, "The heavens are burning, the heavens are burning us up," like a song.

Shaking his fists in anger, a young boy shouted, "We'll get 'em for this!" He was crying and blood oozed from all over his body.

"My wife had a bad gash on her head, but my children had escaped with only scratches."

The elementary school overflowed with injured people. If they couldn't get in, they crouched or lay outside the door. The dead were lined up in the hallways, their bodies disfigured, buried in stench, maggots, and flies. Little pieces of white paper with the names of those who had been identified lay on their stomachs, but there were only a few.

In one classroom an old man lay on his side, curled up like a shrimp in agony. A tiny girl who'd lost her parents was looking around pathetically. There were so many. I walked around looking at each one, but still couldn't find my family. I couldn't think what else to do, so I went back to my home. Again, I found no one.

The sun set and darkness gathered. Exhausted and miserable, I lay down in a clump of marsh grass and gazed at the flames burning the sky red. Questions about my family's fate consumed me.

Then I remembered something. If anything happened, the people in our neighborhood were supposed to go to another elementary school. I couldn't sit still another second. I headed straight for the school.

With the flames burning at my back, I walked more than 10 kilometers on a dark road, praying, "Be there, please be there." I had to drag my painful feet along. But as soon as I set foot in the school I saw them. There they were.

My wife had a bad gash on her head, but my children had escaped with only scratches. Crying, my wife and I grabbed each other's hands.

Night deepened. In pitch darkness I listened to whimpers and groans that seemed to rise from the bowels of the earth. At one point someone struck a match, and a man in the corner panicked. "Put that fire out!" he cried. The match brought back too much of the terror.

The next morning we heard that a military rescue squad had arrived near our home so we decided with two or three other families to go there for help. People were gathering broken, charred boards to make shelters. My wife's head wouldn't stop bleeding, which kept us all worried, but I decided to collect broken boards to make a hut to shelter my family.

Sometimes American B-29 airplanes passed overhead like the one that had dropped the atomic bomb. I had to look for my wife's father and other relatives

53

"Bomb-related diseases have continued to steal away the lives of survivors ever since, even the lives of our children. No A-bomb must ever fall again. We don't need any more survivors."

as well as forage for food. My older sister's family lived closer to the explosion. Their daughter, just turned five, hadn't been hurt at all, but a week later she suddenly developed reddish-black spots all over her body. She vomited blood and died the next day.

My younger sister's husband was a large man. He died four weeks after the bombing, reduced to a greenish-black mummy. In the end, I burned the bodies of seven members of my family who died from the atomic bomb. Everywhere in my neighborhood, soldiers were stacking corpses, covering them with heavy oil so they would burn. And there were other grief-stricken families burning their own loved ones. Day after day the white smoke of cremation rose endlessly, filling the air.

The survivors wandered throughout the city. We ate anything we could put in our mouths, unaware that it was poisoned by radiation. Most of us came down with high fevers and diarrhea. Some died. Truly, living or dying made no difference. It was all hell.

Bomb-related diseases have continued to steal away the lives of survivors ever since, even the lives of our children. No A-bomb must ever fall again. We don't need any more survivors.

Smiles are the Most Important Things We Have

Ms. Toyoko Sugano, 1980

Before the war, Toyoko Sugano taught sewing. Because the military police insisted that all young women participate in the war effort, she entered a women's troop and received military training. At first she worked day and night in a canning factory. Later she was moved to a factory that made military parts and ammunition. Every day for several years she worked sewing clothes for the military.

"All of a sudden I saw a flash. I fainted for several hours, but I don't know how long it truly was. After some time, I woke up because my body hurt so much. It was dark all around me."

At the time of the bombing, Miss Sugano was 23 years old. She recounted her long journey of recovery and her desperate efforts to come to terms with her life. Her fingers were paralyzed so she could no longer sew. She never married, and she felt the pain of discrimination against those who were thought to be infected with "A-bomb disease."

Finally, with the help of a Buddhist monk, she realized that a loving heart could help overcome her terrible memories and face the future. She looked after her sick mother until her death and helped care for the young children in her extended family. She suffered from thyroid and liver problems, and in 1986 she died of a heart attack.

One morning as I was sewing by the factory window, there was an air raid siren. After the warning stopped I began working again. All of a sudden I saw a flash. I fainted for several hours, but I don't know how long it truly was. After some time, I woke up because my body hurt so much. It was dark all around me. Pieces of iron and glass were all over my body, but strangely I didn't feel pain. I saw one very small light somewhere, so I tried to go towards the light.

I didn't know where I was going. I couldn't find any roads because the streets were filled with all kinds of debris and electric poles. I walked and walked, with pain all over my body, thinking that I was dying. I was just wandering around.

I saw somebody whose skin was hanging from their hands and whose tongue was hanging down to their chest. It reminded me of a picture of hell that my grandmother showed me in the Buddhist temple when I was very young. The things I saw were more horrible than anything I had ever seen or heard of hell. People came near me and tried to hang onto me, but most simply fell on the street. They asked me to help them, but I couldn't possibly help those people. I had to leave them. Fires were breaking out everywhere.

I saw one woman just sitting and saying over and over, "Help me, help me." I asked her what was the matter and she told me somebody was under the fallen house and she couldn't possibly help him. She begged for help on her knees, with her forehead on the street. I said, "I'm sorry, I'm sorry." I couldn't help her.

I saw so many people, such terrible looking people, who didn't even look like human beings. Their hair was all red and curled. I remembered when I was a young woman, permanent wave curling came into the beauty parlor and maybe a hot iron fell on them and burned them. These people were burned red and bloody all over, with hair completely burned.

I was almost naked. All my clothes were burned off. I don't know how long I walked, but somehow I reached the river. The fire was coming towards me. I

"The things I saw were more horrible than anything I had ever seen or heard of hell. People came near me and tried to hang onto me, but most simply fell on the street."

59

"Something was touching my face. Then I looked up and saw many dead bodies floating. I don't know whether they were men or women or children."

crawled into the river. The water was so hot! I lowered my head in the water and then I put my face up. There was a wind blowing with the fire and my hair was all burned. So I had to put my head down into the water again.

Something was touching my face. Then I looked up and saw many dead bodies floating. I don't know whether they were men or women or children. Those still alive were moaning and groaning, floating in the river. I thought I was going to die.

I was so hot, so I put my head into the water again. When I looked up, it was already evening. When the fire had burned down somewhat, I climbed to the riverbank and fainted again.

When I woke up it was morning. I was so thirsty, craving for water. Then I noticed that black rain had fallen all over me. I was all black. I wanted to drink something but I didn't have the courage to go down to the river and drink that water. I could see the black rain made black water in a hole in the ground. I drank it because there was nothing else to drink. I drank the muddy water and then I fainted again.

The next time I opened my eyes I was at a grammar school in Hiroshima. I was bloody and burned all over my body. A man came with a rice bowl and gave some rice to me. I was very hungry, so I extended my hand and took the rice and then tried to put it into my mouth. But I couldn't eat because I felt nauseous, even though I was starving. I wanted to drink water but I didn't have the courage to get up. So I lay down on the ground and the afternoon passed and evening came.

I wanted to see my mother, even though I might die. A bone was coming out of my body because the burn was so bad, and it was very painful. A man came and told me, "You should not get up and walk." Anyway, I wanted to see my mother, and since I was born in Hiroshima I knew the area very well.

So I crawled on my hands and knees. When I reached Hiroshima it was already dark. I don't know how long it took. I saw a mountain or a hill or something like that, and I wondered what had happened because it should be burned down and flat, but there was something that looked like a hill. Then I saw it was all the dead bodies, heaps and heaps of dead bodies. Those were heaps of children's bodies, all swollen from the burns.

I sat in front of the heaps of bodies chanting a Buddhist prayer. Some horses nearby were swollen with burns -- their bodies were swollen to two or three times their normal size. They fell on the bodies. Everything was mixed in a heap.

I was determined to see my mother. I don't know how many days it took, but I walked and walked and tried to go to my mother's house. The area where she lived was a suburb of Hiroshima so I had to go to the train station. I fainted

"I wanted to see my mother, even though I might die. A bone was coming out of my body because the burn was so bad, and it was very painful. A man came and told me, 'You should not get up and walk.' Anyway, I wanted to see my mother, and since I was born in Hiroshima I knew the area very well."

61

"My mother had survived! She didn't recognize me because I looked like a ghost. We just hugged each other and wept."

again and again and when I woke up it was already dark. There was water on the ground, so I drank the muddy water and then I crawled again, telling myself if I could go five or six stations farther, then I could see my mother. I thought if I could see my mother then I would be willing to die.

I reached the train station, and then I arrived at a temple. I tried to find a place to sit. I saw a man who looked like he had pieces of rice all over his body. But then I saw they were worms, flies, and larvae. Even though the man was alive, all these worms were coming out of the scars of his burns. That was the only place I could find to sit, so even though there were thousands of worms, I sat there. I felt so sorry for the man.

I wanted to go to the bathroom, and there was a straw curtain there. As I tried to get to the toilet, something touched me. Then I saw a naked body, 19 or 20-year-old girl who had hung herself in the toilet. So I came back and gathered my courage and continued to walk to see my mother.

As I walked, I drank the muddy water and ate some grass in the street. Finally I got to the town where my mother lived. My mother had survived! She didn't recognize me because I looked like a ghost. We just hugged each other and wept. My mother thought that I was dead and she had already prayed in front of the Buddhist altar, burning incense to console my soul.

When I saw my mother's face I was so relieved I collapsed. I couldn't eat anything for several days. Of course, my mother was also badly injured on her leg. But in spite of her own injuries she took care of me. She tried to help me eat, but whenever I put something in my mouth, I threw up. I passed bloody stools. But if I told her, my mother would worry about me, so I kept silent. My nose was bleeding every day and I couldn't stop it. I thought I was dying.

One day I ran a very high fever and my mother asked, "What happened to you?" My hair all fell out, and there were spots all over my body. I told my mother I'd better die. But my mother said, "If you die, I will die too."

My mother found a doctor from town, and he diagnosed me as having diptheria. I was isolated because it is an infectious disease. Somebody said I should have some medicine and they gave me an injection of serum. After that I recovered somewhat, but my health was deteriorated. I finally left the hospital because my mother was also injured and I wanted to see her.

One morning when I woke up I saw smoke. It was around 5:30 or 6 in the morning. I asked my mother, "Mother, are you baking fish this morning? I can't see." When she saw my eyes, she said, "What happened to you? There's no smoke." I said I could see blue and red smoke all over. My mother was shocked. "What happened to your eyes?" I told my mother I couldn't see anything, I could only see smoke.

"One day I ran a very high fever and my mother asked, 'What happened to you?' My hair all fell out, and there were spots all over my body. I told my mother I'd better die. But my mother said, 'If you die, I will die too.'"

63

"For four years I was completely blind. I couldn't do anything, just lie in bed or occasionally sit up. Every morning it was so painful, I felt sad that I'd lived another day."

My mother was so worried. Since we didn't have any transportation, we changed trains many times and went to the eye doctor. There was also a bone sticking out of my leg, but we didn't have medicine to heal that injury. I told my mother to leave me alone. I wanted to die. But my mother insisted that I should see the eye doctor. So we finally went to the doctor. I still couldn't see anything.

We didn't have much to eat at that time because food was very scarce. There was some grass or herbs along the streets and the old people could tell which were good plants and which were poisonous. Our house in the city was completely burned and we didn't have clothes we could exchange for food. So we took the grass in the street and boiled it. We ground it and ate it.

We didn't have money to buy rice or soy sauce, so we asked the rice shop to give us some bran. Whenever I tried to eat the rice bran, I threw up. One sort of herb or plant smelled very bad, but my mother said this is a good plant. She boiled it and put it into my mouth. Even though the plant had a very bad smell, it might have been good for me. I gradually recovered.

For four years I was completely blind. I couldn't do anything, just lie in bed or occasionally sit up. Every morning it was so painful, I felt sad that I'd lived another day.

When I was 27, my left eye suddenly became clear and I could see light. I told my mother, I can see the light! My mother was so glad, she started to cry. And then gradually, strangely, I could walk by myself again. Maybe that stinking grass was good for me! Some people said that no grass would grow for many years. But my mother kept telling me that this grass was good, so maybe it saved my life.

I couldn't get married. I didn't have my youth. When I was around 30 years old, an arranged marriage was offered to me. The man who had arranged the marriage asked me if I had been exposed to the A-bomb. And since I was quite innocent, I told him yes. He said the A-bomb is infectious and he ran away from the scene. He just stood up and left!

I didn't know that the A-bomb was infectious, and when I came back home I asked my mother. We didn't know anything about it. I thought that when I was trying to find my mother, maybe I took in all of the poisons of the A-bomb and maybe it was infectious. I was so disappointed and depressed because I was told that I could never get married.

Some people said that they would introduce me to men that I could marry, but I myself believed that I was infectious and I didn't want to expose myself to that embarrassment. Then I read an article in the newspaper that said if you get married and bear children then the children will have serious diseases. So I gave up getting married.

"When I was around 30 years old, an arranged marriage was offered to me. The man who had arranged the marriage asked me if I had been exposed to the A-bomb. And since I was quite innocent, I told him yes. He said the A-bomb is infectious and he ran away from the scene."

65

"I wanted to commit suicide several times. But whenever I tried, I was saved. I don't know why I was living, but I couldn't die."

I was asked to help in the shop of a relative who had cancer while she was in the hospital. After several years I changed jobs, and in the new office I had several girlfriends. We were very friendly, and they were very gentle and kind to me. One time, three of my girlfriends asked me to go to the coffee shop. Since we were such good friends, we were just chatting and listening to music. Then they served us glasses of water. The waitress forgot to bring me a glass of water and I was very thirsty. My friend was drinking her water, and I asked her to let me drink from her glass. When I drank her water, I sensed that my three friends were quietly looking at each other.

When I returned the glass of water to my friend and said thank you, she said, "Well, you were A-bombed, and I don't want to drink out of your glass." I was shocked because everybody thought I was infectious even though we were such good friends. I didn't know what to do. Nothing was working out, I was all by myself, and I couldn't understand why I had to suffer so much.

I wanted to commit suicide several times. But whenever I tried, I was saved. I don't know why I was living, but I couldn't die. Since we didn't have much money, I had to work because my mother was bedridden. Whenever I tried to commit suicide, every time I wanted to die, my mother's face came to my mind. If my mother had not been with me, I don't know what I would have done. I *couldn't possibly kill myself. I don't know why we had to suffer like this for so long. What is life to me? It has been such a painful life.*

I was told that some people were suffering more than we did. At that time I didn't believe in God, I didn't believe in Buddha, because I didn't know why God had given me such a painful life. My ancestors were Christians.

I didn't want to show my sad face to my mother because she was very ill. Everybody wants to get married, and if you can never marry, you get depressed. So naturally I always had a very gloomy expression. My mother could tell how I felt and she was gloomy too. So I felt sorry for her and maybe I wanted to see a smile on her face.

I went to the temple to say a prayer for those who were killed in the war. A priest came to me and said, "You look very sad. What happened to you?" The Buddhist monk told me many people who are suffering have lots of sad memories. But he told me that those who cannot please their parents are the most undutiful children. He told me to come back again. And then, gradually, very slowly, my mind started to open. My mother suffered from a number of A-bomb diseases, but since I took care of her so well, her face was beautiful when she died. She had a smile on her face. So gradually I opened my mind to the world. I think this is very important. Smiles are the most important things we have.

"I didn't want to show my sad face to my mother because she was very ill."

67

"I walk along the streets, but every time I reach a certain point, I still remember the thousands of corpses, the people like ghosts. I can never forget."

I can never forget the terror that I saw, the thousands of burned bodies and the fires when I was in the river. It was more frightening than hell. I still remember the voice of a woman screaming. The fire came all over the river, and those screams were coming from human beings who were burned alive.

Every time I see anything…for example, we have a beautiful city. I walk along the streets, but every time I reach a certain point, I still remember the thousands of corpses, the people like ghosts. I can never forget. Every time I awake in the morning I still remember these terrible figures.

At that time I was young and beautiful. Then the A-bomb was dropped and changed my life. I was innocent. I didn't commit any crime. I don't know why it destroyed my life.

When I was young I resented the United States because it prevented me from getting married, from falling in love. I had such a narrow mind. I really wanted to go to the United States and drop the A-bomb there when I was young. I'm sorry about that.

A-bombs should be eliminated, by all means. I think all countries should get together and be friendly. If all countries were friends, I think there would be no A-bombs.

I think for the sake of everybody in the world, A-bombs should not exist. In Christianity you say you should love your neighbors and you should love your enemies. I think the most important thing is love. I don't care whether it's Christianity or Buddhism or what kind of religion, we should spread this religion of love to stop the terrible experience of the A-bomb. We should hold hands with people all over the world with smiles on our faces. I think this is the only way that we can have peace.

I think it's extremely difficult for other people to understand someone like me. For example, what is falling in love to the person who has never fallen in love? Patience, effort, and courage, I think these three things are needed to help you understand. And love, you need love.

"We should hold hands with people all over the world with smiles on our faces. I think this is the only way that we can have peace."

The Colors Are Thick in My Paintings

Mr. Tsutomu Masuda, 1980

Born in 1916, Mr. Tsutomu Masuda worked first as a teacher, but decided to train as an artist in Tokyo. In failing health, however, he returned to Hiroshima, where he became an art teacher.

He was a teacher at Daiichi Elementary School when the atomic bomb was dropped. He was leading a group of 150 girls from the school, helping them tear down buildings to make firebreaks at the foot of Hijiyama Bridge. Seriously burned by the explosion, he watched his 18-month-old son die that night from radiation poisoning.

71

He resumed his career as an educator, retiring in 1976 as principal of Hiroshima's Kannon Junior High School. He began painting again, producing more than 1,000 paintings depicting the impact of the atomic bomb. Driven by the memories of his dying students, he devoted his life to exploring the meaning of the atomic bombing through his art.

When the bomb was dropped, the girls were scattered in all directions. Some of them came to me with raised arms crying, Help, help! Their voices still ring in my ears. Their hair was wild, their faces smudged with dust and dirt. What a miserable sight to see in a single second! Who could have ever imagined such a living hell!

Girls swept away by the flowing river, girls crawling into bomb shelters only to die, girls reaching home and dying in agony within a few days -- about 50 of my students died right before my eyes.

Many people caught under fallen buildings were burned to death in the flames. Babies would feel for their dead mothers' breasts. Many more, thirsting for water, tried to pull themselves into water tanks and breathed their last.

Wounded and burned myself, I escaped about ten miles out into the countryside

and lay unconscious for nine days. They tell me
that I kept saying, Give me water, give me water!
I was confined to my bed for a month and it took
two more months before I was strong enough to
go to see my school.

That was my experience of the atomic bomb.
The years have not washed away the shock I
experienced at that time. It is still in me.

After several years, I started painting. At first I
chose other subjects -- I painted mountains and
flowers. But essentially I had to draw scenes
of the atomic bombing. My intention was not
simply to record the atomic bombings, but rather
to think about that time and make an artistic
expression of my experience.

My paintings are not a documentary record of the atomic bomb experience.
They are a creative expression of my own experiences. I believe that whether this
is a beautiful picture or not is rather trivial, in a sense. I believe that a written
record, although it is important, may not reach the depth that is necessary to fully

NIGHT

Night has come
Night has come
Bringing pain, anger
and sadness.   73

CROWS THAT SURVIVED

Burned yet still standing
trees embrace and
hope lives.

74

describe something. So I condensed all these things into my paintings and poems.

The atrocities and tragedies created by the atomic bombing are the subjects that I want to communicate. It is not that I want to dwell on the past. But I do hope that those who view my paintings will increase their desire for peace. That is all that I am trying to do. It is the strongest commitment that I have.

The colors are thick in my paintings. Their texture reflects my agony in producing them. Whenever I make a painting, I ask myself if I have expressed truly what I really saw. No matter how many times I try, I cannot really do it. And in the agony of not being able to get it out on canvas, I watch the paintings become thicker and thicker. Still, it is my responsibility to go on trying. It is my mission – as a survivor and an artist.

In Japan, it is said that stones may contain the spirits of people who have passed away. The stones on the riverbank today are the same as they were 60 years ago.

Mr. Tsutomu Masuda

They have not changed over the years. The city itself has changed, but not the stones on the riverbank. These stones saw the bodies of people floating on the river. Now when I look at these stones, which experienced those things, I feel sad, or sometimes I feel angry. Sometimes I feel that the stone is actually somebody's bone.

SOLILOQUY
The stones keep talking,
even now
they are talking. 75

Help Us Be the Last Victims

Mrs. Etsuko Nagano, 2001

Etsuko Nagano told her story to a large group of students and townspeople in Oberlin, Ohio on the eve of September 11, 2001, the night before the tragedy of war was newly brought home to the American people.

As news of the World Trade Center attacks came across the television, Mrs. Nagano was telling her story at a middle school with seventh and eighth graders, the same age she had been at the start of World War II. The students asked her

77

When the bomb hit Nagasaki, it missed its target, Mitsubishi Steel Works, and exploded instead over Urakami Cathedral.

what she thought, and she answered, "I think war is terrible, and I am very sorry. We all hate war."

The world was horrified at the terrible destruction in New York City, where more than 3,000 people died in a few minutes. To put the tragedy in perspective, in Hiroshima more than 100,000 people were killed in an instant, and in Nagasaki more than 75,000 died. In the years that followed, many more died from diseases caused by intense radiation. The total number who have died from bomb-related causes is now estimated at 340,000.

When the bomb hit Nagasaki, it missed its target, Mitsubishi Steel Works, and exploded instead over Urakami Cathedral. Mrs. Nagano was 16 years old. She was in a gymnasium of Nagasaki University making some nuts and bolts, about two miles away.   This is the story she told on September 10, 2001.

At around 11 o'clock on the morning of August 9, we saw a flash and it became dark a split second later. We heard tin roofs and roofing tiles fly through the air outside. The windows of the gym were blown out with the blast, and clouds of dust came in. I covered my eyes and ears with my hands, but I felt dust in my mouth. I lay down on the floor. The blast was so strong I couldn't open my eyes.

After a while I fled to an air raid shelter nearby. I stayed there for a few hours, and then a factory worker came to me and asked if I was from the Urakami district. He heard that the whole town was destroyed, so I should go check on my family.

The factory that I was working in at that time was behind some hills, so we didn't have such severe damage there. I hurried to check on my family who were all much closer to the explosion.

When I got to Nagasaki train station, I could look out over the neighborhood, and I saw scorched fields, burnt-out ruins, debris everywhere. All the buildings and houses were burned down or destroyed. I couldn't walk straight to my house, so I decided to follow a railroad track to get home.

I walked about a mile following the railroad track, and then I came to a point where I should make a right turn. My house was ten minutes away. But there was no way to go there because the streets were covered with debris. So I made a left turn and tried to cross a bridge.

At the bridge, I ran into my father who was hurrying home from one of the Mitsubishi factories. At that point I had no idea what had happened. I knew it was a bomb but I didn't know anything about atomic bombs and I didn't know where the explosion had been.

"When I got to Nagasaki train station, I could look out over the neighborhood, and I saw scorched fields, burnt-out ruins, debris everywhere. All the buildings and houses were burned down or destroyed."

79

"People roaming on the streets staggered towards us and said, 'please give us some water, please help us' but I didn't have a canteen or anything with me, so we couldn't help them."

My father and I came to a second bridge and there I saw a dead horse. It looked like it was burned instantly. It was all charred black, and was still standing. Then we saw a black mound -- it looked like two people together, a mother and a baby. They were leaning towards a kitchen sink. The house was gone, so I could see those two burnt figures together, leaning on a sink.

I looked around and saw another big building of Mitsubishi Steel Works at the end of the bridge, and it was on fire. I could see the steel reinforcing bars of the building were bent like candy. The inside of the building was hollow because of the fire.

I saw many dead bodies scattered all over the ground. Some of them were charred and others were beheaded skeletons. Humans and animals were dead, everywhere.

Many people roamed the streets, some of them had skin hanging down in shreds from the burns. I saw a man whose skin was hanging from his fingers, and he was lifting his arms out in front of him so that it was less painful. My father and I were probably the only people there who were not harmed. I also saw some people whose eyes had popped out. People had burns all over.

People roaming on the streets staggered towards us and said, "please give us some water, please help us," but I didn't have a canteen or anything with me, so we couldn't help them. They were dying right in front of me. I saw 30 or 40 people die on the spot.

Since the buildings around us were all on fire, we couldn't easily get to our house. So we decided to spend the night in one of the nearby air raid shelters and go on the next morning. Inside there were no candles, no electricity, complete darkness. As I was sitting there I heard enemy fighters flying outside and I heard -- bam bam -- loud noises. I thought it was a gas tank exploding. Later somebody told me it was actually oil drums bursting. The sound was echoing outside and it felt like a living hell. I won't be able to forget all these noises and scenes all my life.

The next morning my father and I continued our walk home. Smoke was still coming up from the ground. As far as I could see, there was nothing but burnt ruins. I saw charred bodies, more beheaded skeletons, more dead animals. We walked forward, being careful not to step on the dead bodies. When we finally got home, where our house had stood there was nothing. I saw a blackened body, and I thought it was my mother. I started crying, saying, "Mother, Mother." My father said, "Where are your brother and sister? Let's go find them."

At that point, a friend of mine from the neighborhood passed by and she said, "Oh, Etsuko, I saw your brother in an air raid shelter. Go help him. I'm sorry I

"As far as I could see, there was nothing but burnt ruins. I saw charred bodies, more beheaded skeletons, more dead animals."

81

"He could neither see nor speak. But this little child nodded. So I asked again, 'Are you really Seiji, my brother?' And he nodded again."

couldn't do anything to help him yesterday."

There were several shelters nearby so we checked each one of them, calling his name. My brother's name was Seiji. Finally after visiting three or four shelters I saw a boy of about the same height as my brother and I called to him, "Are you Seiji?" The boy's face was so swollen like a balloon that he couldn't open his eyes, and he couldn't open his mouth. He could neither see nor speak. But this little child nodded. So I asked again, "Are you really Seiji, my brother?" And he nodded again.

I still didn't want to believe that he was my brother. He was in such terrible condition. But he had an identification tag sewn onto his shirt on his chest, and it said Seiji Kanazawa, 9 years old, fourth grader at the primary school, blood type B. Looking at that tag, I finally realized that it really was my brother. I wondered how he got to the shelter by himself and had to spend the night surrounded by strangers. He was only nine. I was lucky to run into my father on the bridge, but Seiji had to spend the night by himself.

I asked him, "Where are Mother and Kuniko, our sister?" He shook his head. He couldn't see or speak but he could hear. I thought that since he could hear me, he was probably conscious enough to feel pain from his burns.

My father and I decided to take him to a makeshift relief station nearby. But when my father tried to pick him up, he was burned all over and his skin was peeling off, and he couldn't hold him. So my father went outside and from the ruins he found a shutter door and we used it as a stretcher to carry him.

At the relief station, the only treatment that they could provide was some zinc oxide to help the inflammation subside. They had nothing else, no bandages or syringes.

As we were going to another air raid shelter, we met my mother and sister who were coming down from a mountain where they had been hiding. When my mother saw Seiji, my little brother, she burst into tears and cried frantically. She said, "Oh, you must have been really hot, you must be in great pain. I'm sorry, I'm so sorry."

According to my mother, that morning there was no air raid alarm so my brother had asked, "Can I go outside to catch some dragonflies?" He was outside when they saw the flash. My mother and sister were inside the house, and the house collapsed instantly. Finally they managed to get out of the pile of debris.

Two days later on August 11, my brother Seiji passed away in great pain. I believe he felt finally at ease after he heard his parents' voices, and he died. My father took his body outside and we put together about ten bodies on the ground, with some pieces of wood from the ruins, and we cremated them ourselves.

"Two days later on August 11, my brother Seiji passed away in great pain. I believe he felt finally at ease after he heard his parents' voices, and he died."

"On August 15, the long war was ended and all the survivors held each other and wept. Why did we have the war?"

What I remember vividly is the smell. I remember the smell of people burning their family members' dead bodies. I also remember some rescue groups brought rice balls for us to eat but some of them were rotting, and I still remember that smell. Also with the rice balls they brought some pickled vegetables, and together with all those smells I still remember that the dead bodies were everywhere on the ground and they were all rotting.

On August 15, the long war was ended and all the survivors held each other and wept. Why did we have the war? I couldn't stop my tears when I thought about the countless number of people who were killed and their families were in deep sadness. If we had to be defeated anyway, why couldn't the end of the war have come earlier? If the war had ended earlier, the atomic bombs might not have been dropped on Hiroshima or Nagasaki. Many more people would have survived. I couldn't help thinking about it.

On the following day, my family decided to go to a small town where my father was originally from, so we walked there. My mother held a rice ball that she found in the ruins where she put my brother Seiji's ashes. She held it next to her chest. We walked and slept outside overnight. We kept walking for several days.

Even after we arrived, my sister would cover herself with a futon whenever she heard planes flying outside. One month later, on September 10, my sister passed away from radiation sickness. She was in great pain for the last week. We heard a rumor that if you drank water from a well, you would get sick. Some people said that when you lose your hair, that's one of the symptoms of radiation sickness. My sister lost her hair, her gums were bleeding and she had purple spots all over her body.

My mother became very ill a week later after my sister died. She was seriously dehydrated, so she was hospitalized for a month. Finally she recovered, and she lived 50 years after that. However, every day she would say, I wish I were dead, thinking of her two children.

I cannot find any good words to describe how I felt when I lost my siblings. Losing your loved ones is such a terrible thing. I may look healthy, but even after so many years I still have a large scar in my mind.

When the war broke out in 1942, my brother and sister had been sent away because it was a common practice in those days to send younger children to the countryside. They were there for about a year. I missed them so I asked my mother if I could visit them. My mother said, "Yes, you can visit them but don't force them to come home, because if they want to stay there, they should stay." I went to see my brother and sister. They said, "We've made friends here so we want to stay." But I said, "Don't you want to see your mother? And in case

"I cannot find any good words to describe how I felt when I lost my siblings. Losing your loved ones is such a terrible thing. I may look healthy, but even after so many years I still have a large scar in my mind."

85

"I firmly believe that we must not have war. We should not develop nuclear weapons and we must not have any wars that will involve nuclear weapons. "

something terrible happens we should all die together as a family." So I forced them to come back to Nagasaki.

That was at the end of March in 1945. Only a few months later my brother and sister were killed because of the bombing. Even now, I still cannot feel completely happy. I have a feeling of guilt. I feel sorry for my brother and sister and for my parents who lost two children. I felt so upset that I even thought about committing suicide. But I held out against the temptation because I needed to take care of my mother.

After the atomic bombs were dropped there was a rumor that no plants would grow for seven years, but surprisingly the next spring I saw grasses and trees blooming, although some were crooked.

Both cities were rebuilt eventually, but the people who died are gone forever. I firmly believe that we must not have war. We should not develop nuclear weapons and we must not have any wars that will involve nuclear weapons.

For fifty years I never talked about my experience with the atomic bomb, even with my family. However, at the fiftieth anniversary of the bombing I felt that I should be thankful that I'm still healthy, and I decided to become a storyteller to tell my story to children. I joined the Nagasaki Association for the Promotion of Peace. Since then, I've spoken to young people about my experience of the atomic bomb.

When I became a storyteller my mother was very happy and I felt I was doing something important for my parent as her child. My husband is also an atomic bomb survivor. He lost his parents, sister, and brother all at once.

A while ago, I had an opportunity to talk to the president of Nagasaki University. I asked him, "What's the course of illness from atomic bombs? For example, my sister died a month later but my mother lived for 50 years." He said, "I had a similar experience. My elder brother died soon after but I'm still healthy. Even after years of studies there is no medical explanation for radiation sickness. We don't know how people become sick from radiation, and we don't have any remedy for the illnesses."

I believe we should never develop nuclear weapons that cause such terrible illnesses. You may not have experienced any wars, but please imagine how terrible it would be if your mother or your friends died burning or your children were killed.

I would like to say, please help us be the last victims of the atomic bombs. We don't want anybody in this world to suffer the agony that we have been experiencing. We are dying, so we need the next generation to know these stories. We would like all people in the world to hear our stories.

To close, I would like to call for the abolition of nuclear weapons and pray that this world will be one without war, only peace.

"We don't want anybody in this world to suffer the agony that we have been experiencing. We are dying, so we need the next generation to know these stories."

This Bitter Memory

Ms. Keiko Murakami, 2005

On December 8, 1941, the Japanese army attacked Pearl Harbor. After that, the Japanese people had to support the Emperor's military forces and to give up all sorts of comfort for the war effort.

In the spring of 1942, Keiko Murakami entered kindergarten at a public elementary school located beside Hiroshima Castle. Nearby were a large number of troops, said to be the heart of the Japanese army. The town was filled with

89

They went back to Hiroshima at the beginning of May, and in June her baby sister was born. Keiko was 8 years old.

soldiers and horses. The children had to sing and dance to cheer up the soldiers, and send origami and paintings to those who were to be sent to battle. Clothing and food were rationed

Many places in Japan had been bombed, but Hiroshima had not been targeted. It was expected, however, that some day the city would be attacked, so older people, women and children were evacuated.

Keiko, her brother and her mother (who was pregnant) went to live with her grandparents in the country. Keiko's father was secretary-general of the volunteer army headquarters in Hiroshima, where he stayed in a hotel.

Keiko's grandfather was a carpenter. He did not have much land for growing vegetables, so there was very little food to share among many relatives. It was especially hard for Keiko's mother. She decided to go back to the city, saying, "We may have bombs dropping on us, but it will be much better for the family to be together." They went back to Hiroshima at the beginning of May, and in June her baby sister was born. Keiko was 8 years old.

Few children remained in Hiroshima. School buildings were confiscated for the army. Every day they took part in air raid drills, collected used tea leaves to feed the horses, grass to feed people, and horse manure for fuel.

August 6, 1945 was a very hot day. There had been an air raid the night before, so everybody had to stay in shelters and nobody had a good sleep. That morning Keiko's father stayed home later than usual, and her mother was preparing breakfast. She casually said to her father that she did not want to go to school that day. He was normally very strict, but he gave her permission to stay home.

Keiko was inside, reading a magazine with her brother. Her father yelled from the yard, "I hear a plane!" She and her brother ran outside to look.

Suddenly my father shouted, "That's not the sound of a Japanese plane. It's dangerous! Run and get in the shelter." My brother and father and I rushed into the shelter built inside the house. The next moment I felt a strong shock. The three of us were caught under the fallen house and we could see a small bit of sky above us. My brother and I clung to our father's waist and together we crawled out of the ground.

We yelled for our mother as loud as possible. Soon we saw the rubble under our feet moving and our mother appeared, holding our baby sister in her arms, two months old.

Mother looked like a mass of blood. Many pieces of glass were stuck all over her

"The next moment I felt a strong shock. The three of us were caught under the fallen house and we could see a small bit of sky above us."

91

"We walked to the river nearby and lay down in the shade of a bush. Many people rushed to the riverbank. They were badly hurt, with their flesh melting and drooping because of their burns."

body. Her right eyeball had popped out and was hanging down to her breast. My father lifted her eyeball in his palm, but he couldn't do anything with it. Then he tore it off and threw it away. He also had serious injuries on his left shoulder. So he took his shirt off, and tied his arm with it to stop the bleeding.

We walked to the river nearby and lay down in the shade of a bush. Many people rushed to the riverbank. They were badly hurt, with their flesh melting and drooping because of their burns. They were tossing their bodies in great suffering, walking around groaning like animals and crouching down in silence. It was a Babel of agonies and cries.

My father tried to bury the body of my baby sister. He thought she had stopped breathing, and he wanted to clean her blood-covered body at least, before cremating her. But at the moment he roughly washed my sister, she gave a feeble cry and came back to life, which was just a miracle.

She needed milk at once. My mother's milk had stopped, due to her great shock. My father dipped a piece of cloth into the river water and tried to get my sister to suck it, but she turned her face away.

My father found a woman whose torn blouse was wet with milk. He begged her to give her milk to my sister, but she said, "My milk belongs to my child, who has just died right now. I shall never give it to any strangers." My father kneeled down on the ground and begged her again and again. However she wouldn't listen to him.

Even dying people around her also raised their voices, saying, "Your dead baby will never come back, but you can save this living baby. Please give your milk to her." Finally, the woman offered her milk to my baby sister and she was saved.

The city was burning, with flames reaching to the sky, and the midsummer heat added to our hunger and thirst, which made it difficult for us even to breathe. No one came to rescue us from anywhere.

After sleeping in the open, my parents decided that my brother and I should be taken to my grandfather's house in the countryside. I had to walk naked, coaxing my crying brother, with my bare feet stepping on the debris in the street, which was scorching hot.

I walked with care, but I sometimes stepped on dead bodies under the debris. That feeling on the soles of my feet comes back to me vividly, even now after half a century. I will have to carry this bitter memory all my life.

About two months after the bombing, I suddenly started to suffer from a high fever, with bloody stools and urine. Doctors had not been informed of symptoms caused by an atomic bomb. Medicine was scarce and my doctor diagnosed

"I walked with care, but I sometimes stepped on dead bodies under the debris. That feeling on the soles of my feet comes back to me vividly, even now after half a century."

"Many women who were pregnant had premature births or stillbirths. There were many cases of premature births or stillbirths even among women who got pregnant later on, and many cases of children with birth defects."

my disease as a serious infection. I had to stay in bed without any treatment. I recovered from the high fever in a month or so, but stinking pus kept oozing out of my ears. All I could do was wipe it off.

When winter came, we returned to Hiroshima and our family was reunited. I was able to go to the Red Cross Hospital, where I learned that my high fever and ear problem had been caused by radiation from the bomb. It was called radiation disease. My symptoms gradually took a turn for the better, thanks to penicillin that we procured on the black market.

Conditions after the war became more tragic than at the time of the bombing. Many women who were pregnant had premature births or stillbirths. There were many cases of premature births or stillbirths even among women who got pregnant later on, and many cases of children with birth defects.

Many survivors had to wear long-sleeved clothes or scarves on their heads or necks, even in the heat of midsummer, to hide ugly scars that formed on their skin where they had sustained bad burns. Some people suffered from radiation disease, and as well as many who were exposed to the black rain. Some people were scared to be in contact with radiation disease survivors.

Many survivors felt uneasy and expected that it might be their turn to suffer next. Some gave up getting married, out of fear of genetic defects caused by radiation.

Some gave up having children.

Those of us who had these experiences came to believe that there should be no more victims of nuclear weapons in the future. It is our mission to give a warning all over the world. However, the United States and other countries still possess nuclear weapons. Japan also has many nuclear power plants, even though disastrous accidents have taken place repeatedly. The fact that the weak are always sacrificed is a hard reality.

The United States used depleted uranium weapons in the Gulf War in 1991. Symptoms similar to those in Hiroshima and Nagasaki have been observed there. Then the United States attacked Iraq again in 2003.

A photography exhibition about the war in Iraq was held in my town. The frightened citizens, injured children or children with sad eyes whose parents were killed, were just like me in 1945. Those children will have to carry these negative memories for the rest of their lives, just as I still have the memory of Hiroshima that never vanishes from my mind.

The present world situation cannot stop me from speaking out against war and nuclear weapons, even as I am getting older. I hope people who meet me will love peace. When a chain of love is made by all people, I am sure a heaven on earth will be built.

"The United States used depleted uranium weapons in the Gulf War in 1991. Symptoms similar to those in Hiroshima and Nagasaki have been observed there. Then the United States attacked Iraq again in 2003."

To Feel Each Other's Pain

Dr. Nobumasa Kimura, 1988

Dr. Nobumasa Kimura is a psychiatrist and a survivor of the atomic bombing in Hiroshima. In his private clinic he treats many survivors, talking to them about their fears and troubles. Dr. Kimura does not talk much about his own experiences, but concentrates on helping others cope with their daily lives and memories.

As a director of the Hiroshima City Medical Association, Dr. Kimura helped write a history of the medical association's efforts to treat bomb survivors. Many local doctors were not allowed to evacuate and remained in Hiroshima throughout the war. They fell prey, one after another, to the effects of the bomb while caring for its victims. They share the suffering of the survivors.

Dr. Kimura had surgery for a rare intestinal cancer caused, he believes, by high doses of radiation he received from the atomic bomb more than 50 years earlier. He is a member of International Physicians for the Prevention of Nuclear War and has talked about his experiences with doctors in China and Russia.

"We were eating breakfast, all seven of us including my aunt and cousin, at a big table. Suddenly the yard flashed yellow. I lost consciousness."

I was eight years old at the time. My mother, sister, and I were staying in a hut west of Hiroshima to avoid the air raids at night. On August 6, we went back to town to have breakfast with our grandparents. We were eating breakfast, all seven of us including my aunt and cousin, at a big table. Suddenly the yard flashed yellow. I lost consciousness.

When I woke up, it was all dark and silent. My left arm was pinned under a post in the collapsed house. My mother and grandfather lifted it and pulled me to the roof, but the roof was on the ground. It was originally a three-story house!

The dust was thick, and I could hear the ground rumbling. My grandfather yelled to help us, and told us to hurry to a safer area. We went to the river, but there was no bridge left. We had to jump pole-to-pole to cross the river. Many people

– you couldn't tell whether they were alive or dead -- were lined up at the river like seals. It was dark. My mother was holding my hand. We asked everyone if anyone had seen my sister, who had been wearing a pink dress. We looked all over. I was so tired.

Many people looked just like the skinned rabbit in the tale of the white hare of Inaba [a Japanese folk legend, in which a hare was skinned by a group of vicious crocodiles]. My mother was about to lose her mind. We frantically looked for my sister, to no avail. We were sitting at the bottom of a hill when a heavy rain started to fall. This was black rain.

Then we met someone who had seen my sister, so my mother took off to find her. I watched the entire town burning. I vividly remember this. Now whenever I see fireworks at the annual fireworks festival, I can't help feeling the same fear again. My heart aches.

We took refuge in a hut in the mountains, since our house in town was demolished. We slept there at night, with no roof. I remember watching the pretty stars in the sky.

Hiroshima was still a sea of fire and the heat was so intense we couldn't walk around. We thought our grandfather would come back after rescuing our grandmother, but he did not come for two days. So we waited a few more

"Now whenever I see fireworks at the annual fireworks festival, I can't help feeling the same fear again. My heart aches."

99

"Rumors spread that we had been attacked by a new type of bomb, and that no plants would grow for 75 years."

days and then went to our house and found both of our dead and scorched grandparents. I was devastated. My grandfather was a faithful Buddhist. He used to tell us he would live to age 61 like Nichiren, a well-known priest. He died with his hands folded as if praying – he was 61.

We stayed a few weeks in the mountains since we no longer had a home to return to. Lots of blisters like chickenpox appeared on my body and festered. I also lost my hair. We watched our town's citizens dying, one after another. Many had purple spots on their skin.

Rumors spread that we had been attacked by a new type of bomb, and that no plants would grow for 75 years. The B-29 airplanes flew so low, I wondered why. Then we learned of Japan's surrender. I heard that the big American soldiers would come and kill children by squeezing them between their legs. I was scared!

We left for the town where my great aunt lived. We went part of the way by train, but the bridge was destroyed so we had to walk the rest of the way. We stayed in a spare room, about 9 feet by 9 feet, that belonged to another family. All of us came down with high fevers. Many people, including one of my cousins, died. The corpses were cremated by the riverside. I was so afraid that all of us would die.

Then my uncle came home from the Japanese Navy. He had medicines and gave a shot to my aunt, and she recovered. I was astonished. By the end of August, my father came home from Manchuria. I remember him standing there with a large backpack on his back.

My father covered a brick room at a soy sauce brewery with a tin roof. We lived there a few years. All of Hiroshima was reduced to ashes. Everyone complained of symptoms.

In 1951, my father died of stomach cancer, and we fell into lives of hardship. We lost our house. My mother opened a cigarette shop. Eventually I managed to go to Hiroshima University.

We were constantly afraid of being discriminated against if we told others we were atomic bomb survivors. Because of the many new cases of leukemia in the 1950's, we were told to keep secret that we'd been exposed to the bomb.

I was a medical student by then, and I kept my eye on the medical reports. The biggest worry of the survivors is bomb-related illnesses. We might develop cancer, cataracts, or other disorders. We may be doing fine so far, but we don't know about the future. This has been agonizing for us.

Our greatest fear is about heredity. Radiation changes genes – we know that. The reproductive organs are most affected and this makes people constantly worried. So far, there are not many cases of birth defects, but lots of cases of sterility or infertility.

"The biggest worry of the survivors is bomb-related illnesses. We might develop cancer, cataracts, or other disorders. We may be doing fine so far, but we don't know about the future."

101

"Even the Atomic Bomb Casualty Commission has recognized the statistical correlation between the amount of radiation exposure and the occurrence of breast and thyroid cancer. This spurred another wave of fear among the survivors."

Then came other occurrences of cancer. The universities and research institutes did not recognize the cancers as significant at the time. But we medical practitioners in Hiroshima took it upon ourselves to take the problem seriously. Using our own private resources, we continued to study. The occurrence of cancer became most noted around 1955. Even the Atomic Bomb Casualty Commission has recognized the statistical correlation between the amount of radiation exposure and the occurrence of breast and thyroid cancer. This spurred another wave of fear among the survivors.

This coincided with a period when those of us who were exposed to the atomic bombs as children became eligible to get married. Certainly marriage is one of the biggest events in life. During that period the genetic effects of the atomic bomb were hotly debated in Japanese families, in Hiroshima and Nagasaki especially. Some people came to the conclusion that they should deny that they had anything to do with the atomic bombs.

I decided I would not marry another A-bomb survivor, and so I married a girl who came from another city far away from Hiroshima. It was only after we were married that I discovered she was also a survivor! She had been a baby in Hiroshima when the bomb was dropped, and her parents moved away when she was young. So I married an A-bomb survivor after all! We have three grown daughters, who have all been healthy, thank goodness.

In Hiroshima after the war, the biggest topic within families was the experiences they had at the time of the bombing and afterward. Of course, the massive destruction of the atomic bomb was mentioned. Even healthy people feel this fear. They wonder what kind of disorders they may face in the future. The more they speak about it, the more they suffer. So they can't talk about it. These are their innermost feelings. I feel the same way.

Post-traumatic stress disorder is also occurring among the survivors. They can't express their feelings, so we have no real data. They lock up their feelings. They have flashbacks and other symptoms of intense psychological stress, which can be triggered by outside events and can arise many years after the initial trauma.

Up until that time, mental illness, which I observed among many people I treated, was caused by great shocks. In this instance the shock was the atomic bombing and the deaths of their husbands, family members, and children. That was the cause of the acute symptoms that I observed.

But greater than that was the fear caused by the aftereffects. This fear was spurred by the occurrence of leukemia in the 1950's. Certainly leukemia is not a

"They wonder what kind of disorders they may face in the future. The more they speak about it, the more they suffer. So they can't talk about it."

103

"Most survivors are reluctant to talk to non-survivors about their experiences. Sometimes they feel strongly that others will think they're asking for pity or they're asking for some kind of compensation."

common disease; its occurrence is rather limited. When people started to observe leukemia, and many cases were found in Hiroshima, it made them fear that they too might get leukemia and related diseases. Leukemia occurs as a result of genetic mutations within the bone marrow. This is evidence that the atomic bombs actually caused some changes in the genes. That's the reason for their fear.

What we are really interested in is the future happiness of each person, no matter what kind of treatment methods we use. As a result we constantly try to collect scientific data concerning the genetic effects caused by the atomic bombings. The doctors and medical associations constantly try to keep up to date. In the course of everyday treatment, we disseminate this scientific data and its implications to our patients.

To feel each other's pain is the essence and the beginning of any treatment. Most survivors are reluctant to talk to non-survivors about their experiences. Sometimes they feel strongly that others will think they're asking for pity or they're asking for some kind of compensation. As a result they do not normally talk to non-survivors. They're usually on their own.

I believe that human beings are very individualistic. Usually it is impossible for us to understand each other. But I believe that in the case of A-bomb survivors, perhaps they are a little bit closer than among other groups. Compared to non-

survivors, their understanding of each other is stronger.

I don't believe there is any bigger trauma than the atomic bombing. The more you know about this, the more difficult it becomes to understand it. I myself don't feel very comfortable on August 6. That's all I want to say.

If we follow our feelings and don't tell our stories, then the people of the world won't know about these experiences, and they cannot be used to educate the rest of the world.

I think the most important thing is to know the truth. Then you have to make a judgment. Whether the judgment is right or wrong depends on the individual. However, unless you know about something, you can't make a judgment. So I think it's very important to know.

More survivors are dying now, and many are speaking out because they're afraid of losing the stories, the memories. But their true feelings are deeply hidden inside. What helps them most is for us to listen.

In the West, when someone is hurt they often want revenge. In Buddhism, we are taught to forgive. All human beings are weak, so we have to forgive each other. We believe God is everywhere. The gods live together in harmony. We should learn to do the same.

"In the West, when someone is hurt they often want revenge. In Buddhism, we are taught to forgive. All human beings are weak, so we have to forgive each other."

We Must Learn to be Freethinkers

Mr. Hiromu Morishita, 1988

O n August 6, 1945, Hiromu Morishita was in the ninth grade and part of a group of children who were mobilized to tear down buildings for firebreaks. In those days, students were sent to factories or other places to fill the manpower shortage, since most of the men were in the military. He was about one mile from the spot where the atomic bomb exploded. The explosion severely scarred the left side of his face and blew off his ear.

107

A quiet, unassuming man, Mr. Morishita is a calligrapher with three children. He teaches at Hatsukaichi Senior High School. He is President of the Japan Association of Secondary School Teacher Survivors and has been chairman of the World Friendship Center, a peace center in Hiroshima, and President of the Japan Association of Secondary School Teacher Survivors.

"One of my friends found me and asked me how his face looked. The skin was hanging down from his face like a rag. I was too scared to ask him about my own face."

It was just like being thrown into an iron melting pot. My face was burned and I jumped into the river. One of my friends found me and asked me how his face looked. The skin was hanging down from his face like a rag. I was too scared to ask him about my own face.

Climbing up Hijiyama hill, standing at the top, I looked around the city. But there was nothing. All the buildings were in pieces, and fires burned here and there all over the area. I felt numb.

A group of soldiers walked by. All of them had been burned and they were holding their arms out in front of them. They looked like marching ghosts. An old lady began chanting a Buddhist prayer when she saw them.

I tried to reach my home, but on the way the air was so hot, it seemed like an invisible wall in front of me, and I couldn't go any further. Instead I went up to the top of another hill to sit and wait for the fires to cool down.

When I got back to the spot where my house had been, I found everything was burned and only a big stone vase to hold water stood on the corner. I realized that my mother was dead and buried under the ashes there.

I remembered that my father had a friend who lived in a suburb of Hiroshima, and I started walking to his house. On the way I fainted, I was so exhausted. One of the neighbors found me and took care of me for a month. There were eight families staying with them during that time.

One of my aunts who wasn't hurt from the bomb came to see me. But she died within a week. Every day many bodies were cremated on the riverbank, and I thought I would be one of them.

Half a year later, school started in a barracks. My teachers and friends were dead and I was lonesome. I didn't feel very happy to be alive. My parents, friends, memories, my city – everything was gone. The beliefs I had been taught and depended on were no longer possible. With no food, farming all day, my future education seemed a faraway dream.

Many years passed. I finally managed to get a college education and began teaching at a girls high school. When I visited the Peace Museum with my

"Half a year later, school started in a barracks. My teachers and friends were dead and I was lonesome. I didn't feel very happy to be alive."

109

"One member of a Board of Education asked me if textbooks in Japan contained a lot of articles on the atomic bomb. I said yes. But when I got home and checked, I did not see many articles in our textbooks."

students, they said they were scared. I realized then that my face must be very ugly and also scary to my students who had to see me every day. That's when I stopped thinking and talking about my misfortune. I thought by not talking about it, I could forget it.

Years later, one of my friends came to me and asked, "What do high school students think about the atomic bombing?" Babies who were born around 1945 would have been high school students then, and my friend wanted to write about their thoughts. I couldn't answer him. I realized that I had to talk about my experiences because my students would never ask me anything as long as I kept quiet.

In 1964, I traveled to the USA, USSR, and Europe. We told our stories at many schools. High school students and housewives came to listen to us of their own free will. In Japan, they would be told to come. Their positive attitude is something we should learn.

One member of a Board of Education asked me if textbooks in Japan contained a lot of articles on the atomic bomb. I said yes. But when I got home and checked, I did not see many articles in our textbooks. So I thought my story could serve as teaching material.

Younger generations who did not have the experience of nuclear bombing increased, and some survivors in Hiroshima began to feel the need to tell their

Mr. Hiromu Morishita

stories to these students. This was called "atomic bomb education" and later changed to "peace education."

Now, under the name of peace education, we talk about abolishing nuclear weapons and wars. But we also need to broaden our minds and open our eyes to find solutions to poverty, injustice, discrimination, hunger, and so on. We need to learn to be freethinkers, nonconformists, and to lead our lives as individuals instead of following the ideas of others.

A Morning Poem

I wish to welcome a reincarnated morning

For that day only

I would not regret dying.

By Hanji Tsusboi, 1973

Calligraphy by Hiromu Morishita

A Process of Gathering Wisdom

Mr. Akira Ishida, 1988

Akira Ishida was a junior airman in the Japanese army and had the day off on August 6, 1945. He was on a streetcar going to the Miyajima shrine with his elder brother to pray for good luck in the war.

After the war ended, Mr. Ishida became a social studies teacher in a junior high school. He told his students about his experiences, although the Japanese government did not approve.

For six years after the war, the occupation policy of the U.S. government prohibited discussion of Hiroshima and Nagasaki. After 1951, the press code was removed and these experiences were included in textbooks, so school children all over Japan studied them for the first time.

Through the late 1950's and 1960's, the Japanese government opposed such teachings. As a result, textbooks gave very little space to descriptions of Hiroshima and Nagasaki. Before long, more than half of the schoolchildren in Japan did not know what August 6 meant.

Some Hiroshima teachers, sensing their responsibility as survivors, started the Japan Hibakusha Teachers Association, with Mr. Ishida as its chairman. They made vigorous efforts to produce supplemental materials for the schools. "We have to teach children," says Mr. Ishida, "we have to teach everybody, I believe, the reality of Hiroshima and Nagasaki."

In 1976, Mr. Ishida sued the Japanese government and won restitution for his injuries received by the atomic bombing. This important case established the responsibility of the Japanese government to pay for medical treatment for the survivors of the atomic bombs and other war victims. Mr. Ishida was also elected to the Hiroshima prefectural assembly.

Twenty years after the bombing, Mr. Ishida wrote a 450-line poem describing his experiences as a survivor, entitled "Aiko 20 Years." Aiko means to love and to pursue the light. Mr. Ishida died in 2003.

That day was so beautiful.

Brother and I took the streetcar for Koi.

We were packed in like sardines,

And I could move neither my hands nor feet,

Just moving with the sway of people.

The woman driver announced, "Inari-machi, Yamaguchi-cho."

From the streetcar, I saw lots of commuters

Hurrying to their offices with air-raid hoods on their backs,

Wearing puttees or Monpe slacks.

Young girls in rayon clothes

115

Went to work with a slight slouch.
We passed the Chugoku Press Company.
The high advertising tower of Jintan Medicine
Was seen on the right.
It stopped at Hatchobori.
Then, a great flash!
Something seemed to hammer on the top of the streetcar.
Utter darkness!
Complete silence, no sound,
Both man and nature were frozen in fear.
With a start I came to myself,
Hands and feet were heavy, hard to move.
Utter darkness surrounded us.
Many people were lying upon me.
Faint groans of pain were heard.

Trying to move, I struggled.
Gradually dim light enabled me to see
A meter or two ahead.
My army uniform was wet with blood.
Motionless bodies were piled one upon another
On the floor of the streetcar.
"I've got to run away," it occurred to me.
Because of the human protection around him,
My brother wasn't hurt, strangely enough.
Feeling my way to the back door,
I managed to get out.
The street could be seen very faintly.
I smelled strong gas, unbearable.
Spontaneously I covered my nose, eyes, and mouth
As we had been told to.

teach us to live

Quickly, steadily,
Something like the fine ash of a fire
Was falling with a steady sound,
Quickly, steadily.
Suddenly hot wind blew down
And took my army cap away.
I scuttled after it and retrieved it
From under the wreckage of the streetcar.
By and by I could see as far as Kamiya-cho.
Strange!
Like a miracle, nothing could be seen that used to be there.
Very dimly only damaged concrete buildings came into view
Solitarily through the hazy mist.
Roofs, roofs were piled up one on top of the other and crushed.
Everything was gone and killed,
As if human life had stopped breathing....

All the Hiroshima citizens walking on the streets were charred, completely burned. I could not believe that these were once human beings. There were rows and rows of bodies lying on the streets. Walking among these bodies I escaped toward the periphery of Hiroshima. I saw people who were trapped under buildings, burned to death. I went through the raging fire and finally made my way to the suburbs where it was much safer. On August 7, I got to my house in the countryside.

Three weeks later, acute symptoms of atomic bomb disease started to appear. All my hair fell out. Purple spots appeared all over my body. I vomited blood, and also had bloody discharge. On September 7, my brother died; he was exposed to the bomb at the same place as I was. For six months I was mostly unconscious. Finally I regained consciousness. A year later, I was able to stand up on my feet for the first time.

> One morning I wiped my face with a towel as usual
>
> And looked in the hand mirror,
>
> In which I found soft hair,
>
> Like downy hair on part of my bald head.

"Mother, hair is growing again!"
I held a few downy hairs tightly with my fingers.
They looked shiny.
It was said that I would be forever bald-headed,
But by ones and twos…, soft hair was brought back to life.
"I am still alive, mother. My hair is living."
My hair grew!
Joy ran through my body.
I was able to get rid of the shadow of death.

For many years, at least once a year I was hospitalized because of various diseases. Since I was close to the hypocenter, my eyes were affected by so-called "radiation cataracts." I am constantly faced with the possibility of going blind at any time.

I feel it is a miracle that I am still alive, and as a result I ask myself, what are the responsibilities of those who survived? How can we best represent those who died? I always think about these questions.

Mr. Akira Ishida

Hiroshima and Nagasaki were the first tragic experiences of nuclear war the human race has ever faced. In the history of human warfare, this is one of the most cruel experiences that humanity has had.

August 6, 1945 marks the beginning of the nuclear age. To teach about Hiroshima and Nagasaki to the rest of the world is very important, because nuclear weapons are threatening the existence of mankind.

Teaching about Hiroshima and Nagasaki is a process of gathering wisdom so that we can continue to exist on this earth. All humankind must face this collectively, and therefore teaching about Hiroshima and Nagasaki is not just a local issue. It should not be taught as a fact pertinent to a geographical area, but rather it should be taught as part of education for survival.

We teach three things to our children in our peace education efforts. First is the dignity, the importance and preciousness of human life. The A-bomb was one of the most atrocious experiences where human lives were belittled.

The second point is to teach the meaning of human life -- what it means to live -- to fulfill all the potential that was given to us as human beings, and not to choose the catastrophic ways of nuclear weapons.

The third point is that in that cruel living hell, human love did not perish. Parents

"To teach about Hiroshima and Nagasaki to the rest of the world is very important, because nuclear weapons are threatening the existence of mankind."

121

"The world does not destroy itself by accident. It occurs by the acts of human beings, especially governments."

saved their children, teachers sacrificed their lives to save their students. There were many experiences of this kind. No matter what kind of atrocity someone faces, there is always courage, there is always brave love.

Sometimes when we teach the younger generation about the atomic bomb, at first the children cry and don't want to hear about it. As a result, showing movies or photographs and telling stories about these experiences is not enough. These things do not mean that you have really taught, that you have fulfilled your responsibility.

So we have added three more points. One is the tragedy, cruelty, atrocity, and inhumanity of war. The world does not destroy itself by accident. It occurs by the acts of human beings, especially governments. Second, we teach children the causes of war and conflict. Third, we teach them that it is possible to prevent war and achieve peace.

It is also important to give as much data as possible concerning nuclear weapons, as well as the possibility of human extinction. This should be taught not only in Hiroshima and Nagasaki, but all over the world.

Frankly, peace education is not widespread in Japan. The government is rather cold toward peace education. I believe that peace education should be taught from the perspective of people in general, not governments. I believe that peace education should be at the core of the school curriculum.

We have to realize that what happened years ago is not just a matter of the past but should also be seen in the context of today. I was shocked when I went to San Diego and San Francisco and observed the warships and nuclear submarines in those ports. What I saw was nuclearism at sea, meaning the nuclear submarines and warships with nuclear weapons.

In San Diego Bay, right where citizens can see them, are huge submarines and warships that have nuclear weapons on board. The shoreline of San Diego has a huge storage facility for nuclear weapons and military factories where the warships are repaired. This is a daily scene for people living there, but for us it is unimaginable.

The citizens enjoy sunbathing on the beaches and swimming in the sea near those ships. Nearby thousands of cows are being raised and eating the grass. It seems the people of San Diego are not informed of what could happen if there is a nuclear war or accident.

When I had an opportunity to meet and talk with some people in San Diego, their reaction was that their livelihoods depend on the nuclear industry. In order to live today, they have to live with the possibility that tomorrow could bring

"We have to realize that what happened years ago is not just a matter of the past but should also be seen in the context of today."

123

death, what we have experienced in Hiroshima.
    It is now 20 years.
    My brother's death was soon followed by my mother's.
    I have survived them by 20 years.
    I think it wonderful.
    I want to say thank you, loudly
    To some inscrutable grace
    For these 20 years of life.
    Even though the bomb's poison remains deep in my body,
    I have to fight for a second life,
    And live 20 years longer.

Study Guide and Resources for Discussion

Nuclear Facts and Figures

In July of 1945, the United States conducted the world's first nuclear test in the desert of New Mexico. Three weeks later, two atomic bombs were dropped on Hiroshima and Nagasaki, Japan. World War II ended soon after.

Two cities were completely destroyed on August 6 and 9, 1945, by the only nuclear weapons ever used in war. More than 140,000 people in Hiroshima

More than 30,000 nuclear weapons now exist on the earth, each with an explosive power many times greater than the bombs that destroyed Hiroshima and Nagasaki

and more than 70,000 people in Nagasaki were killed instantly, and more than 370,000 have died from the aftereffects of the atomic bombings.

The atomic bombs produced fireballs of 1 million degrees Centigrade, blast of 35 tons per square meter. They generated winds up to 1000 miles per hour, intense radiation and massive clouds of radioactive debris that condensed and fell to the ground as "black rain."

Many people exposed to the atomic bombs later died of radiation-related illnesses such as leukemia and other cancers. There are still approximately 260,000 survivors of the atomic bombings alive today. In Japanese, they are known as "hibakusha," or "bomb-affected persons." The genetic effects of radiation exposure upon future generations are still not fully known today.

More than 30,000 nuclear warheads now exist on the earth, each with an explosive power many times greater than the bombs that destroyed Hiroshima and Nagasaki. The United States has approximately 7,000 long-range nuclear warheads and about 4,000 short-range or operational warheads in reserve, many on hair-trigger alert and ready to be launched on 15 minutes' warning. Russia has roughly 19,500. The strategic forces of Britain, France, and China are considerably smaller, with 200-400 nuclear weapons in each country's arsenal. Pakistan and India have fewer than 100 weapons each. Israel is widely believed to have nuclear weapons, and North Korea exploded a nuclear weapon in October of 2006.

A number of international treaties have been signed to reduce the dangers of nuclear weapons and war.

President Eisenhower proposed the first moratorium on nuclear testing in 1957 as a step toward disarmament.

President Kennedy and Soviet Premier Khruschev negotiated a Limited Test Ban Treaty in 1962 that outlawed nuclear testing in the atmosphere, space, and undersea.

The SALT (Strategic Arms Limitation Treaty) agreements in 1971 and 1979, followed by the START (Strategic Arms Reduction Treaty) agreements in 1991 and 1993, placed limits on US and Russian nuclear weapons.

The Anti-Ballistic Missile (ABM) treaty was signed by President Nixon and Soviet Communist Party Secretary Brezhnev in 1972, but 30 years later President George W. Bush withdrew the U.S. from the treaty.

The Nuclear Non-Proliferation Treaty, negotiated in 1968, required all non-nuclear nations not to develop nuclear weapons, while the nuclear powers agreed to gradually eliminate their nuclear arsenals and provide non-nuclear

The Anti-Ballistic Missile (ABM) treaty was signed by President Nixon and Soviet Communist Party Secretary Brezhnev in 1972, but 30 years later President George W. Bush withdrew the U.S. from the treaty.

Six treaties have declared Africa, Antarctica, Southeast Asia, Australia and New Zealand, Latin America and the Caribbean, and Outer Space to be "nuclear weapon free zones." Not all countries honor these treaties, however.

countries with nuclear technology for peaceful purposes. Efforts by Iran and North Korea to develop nuclear weapons threaten to undermine this treaty.

A Comprehensive Test Ban Treaty outlawing all nuclear weapons tests was ratified by 132 nations in 1996, but some countries including the U.S., China, Israel, North Korea, India, Pakistan, and Iran have not signed or ratified it, so it has not gone into effect.

Only one country has been known to dismantle its nuclear arsenal completely—the apartheid government of South Africa apparently developed a few nuclear weapons, but they were dismantled in the early 1990s. After the fall of the Soviet Union, a number of former Soviet republics (Belarus, Ukraine, and Kazakhstan) found themselves in possession of nuclear weapons, but they gave them back to Russia or dismantled them.

Six treaties have declared Africa, Antarctica, Southeast Asia, Australia and New Zealand, Latin America and the Caribbean, and Outer Space to be "nuclear weapon free zones." Not all countries honor these treaties, however. The danger of nuclear war is far from over, and nuclear weapons are still with us.

Books for Adults

Many books and films have been made about Hiroshima and Nagasaki, from memoirs to fiction. Most are in Japanese, but some are available in English.

The Atomic Bomb: Voices from Hiroshima and Nagasaki (Japan in the Modern World) edited by Kyoko and Mark Selden (M.E.Sharpe, 1997).   Artistic responses to the atomic bombings with poetry, stories, poems, etc.

Black Rain by Masuji Ibuse, translated by John Bester (Kodansha, 1994). Classic novel about a family dealing with life after the atomic bombing.

Children of the Paper Crane: The Story of Sadako Sasaki and Her Struggle with A-Bomb Disease, by Masamoto Nasu, translated by Elizabeth Baldwin, Steve Leeper, and Kyoko Yoshida (M.E. Sharpe, 1996). Biography of the sixth-grade student whose death from leukemia inspired a children's peace movement.

Death In Life: Survivors of Hiroshima, by Robert Jay Lifton (University of North Carolina Press, 1991). This study of "psychic numbing" won a National Book Award in the Sciences in 1969, but its analysis is controversial in Japan.

Duty: A Father, His Son, and the Man Who Won the War, by Bob Greene (Harper, 2001). Memoir of a man coming to terms with his dying father, and a rare conversation with the pilot who flew the atomic bomb to Hiroshima.

The danger of nuclear war is far from over, and nuclear weapons are still with us.

Empire and the Bomb, by Joseph Gerson (Pluto Press, 2007). Masterful analysis of the flaws in the argument that the bomb would save American lives or force an unwilling Emperor to surrender.

Fate of the Earth, by Jonathan Schell (Knopf 1982). Eloquent rethinking of the global impact of the nuclear arms race first published in The New Yorker.

See also The Abolition (Knopf, 1984), Schell's thoughtful plan for disarmament.

Hiroshima, by John Hersey (Vintage, 1989). The first journalistic account of the atomic bombing, originally published by The New Yorker in 1946, remains a classic. See also "Hiroshima: the Aftermath," The New Yorker, July 5, 1985.

Hiroshima and Nagasaki: The Physical, Medical, and Social Effects of the Atomic Bombings, Committee for the Compilation of Materials on Damage Caused by the Atomic Bombings in Hiroshima and Nagasaki, translated by Eisie Ishikawa and David Swain (Basic Books, 1981). Massive compilation of scientific data on the atomic bombs by foremost Japanese experts.

Hiroshima in America: A Half Century of Denial, by Robert Jay Lifton with Greg Mitchell (Quill, 1996). Examination by a psychiatrist and journalist of U.S. government efforts to mold public opinion after the atomic bombings.

Hiroshima's Shadow, edited by Kai Bird and Lawrence Lifschultz (Pamphleteer's Press, 1998). Overview of the history and politics of the decision to use atomic weapons, a comprehensive and critical anthology.

Hiroshima Notes by Kenzaburo Oe, translated by David Swain and Toshi Yonezawa (Grove Press, 1996). Collection of essays by Nobel Prize winning novelist who also wrote The Crazy Iris and Other Stories of the Atomic Aftermath (Grove Press, 1985).

White Flash, Black Rain: Women of Japan Relive the Bomb, edited by Lequita Vance-Watkins and Mariko Aritani (Milkweed, 1995). Women speak of the shared accountability for war: not only the destruction unleashed by the atomic bombs, but also the disastrous path Japan followed in World War II.

Writing Ground Zero: Japanese Literature and the Atomic Bomb, by John Whittier Treat (University of Chicago Press, 1995). Compelling study of Japanese writing about the bomb, from the earliest survivor writers to important Japanese poets and novelists today.

Children's Books

Barefoot Gen, by Keiji Nakazawa (Tokyo, SanYuSha, 1978-9, Penguin Books, 1989, Translated by Project Gen). Four-volume graphic novel that tells the story of Hiroshima in Japanese comic book style. Also available on VHS.

Hiroshima no Pika (Flash over Hiroshima), by Toshi Maruki (Harper Collins, 1980). Beautifully illustrated book about a young girl's experience, with paintings by noted Japanese artist. Won Ehon Nippon Prize for best picture book in Japan. Also available on DVD, narrated by Susan Sarandon.

I want young people to remember that today's elderly survivors were as young as they are when their families, their schools, and their communities were destroyed in a flash.

—Tadatoshi Akiba, Mayor of Hiroshima

<u>Sadako and the Thousand Paper Cranes</u>, by Eleanor Coerr (Puffin, 1999). True story of a young girl who died of leukemia as a result of radiation from the bomb. Also adapted as a picture book by Coerr and Caldecott award-winning illustrator Ed Young (Paper Star, 1997) for ages 8-12.

<u>Shin's Tricycle</u>, by Tatsuharu Kodama (Walker & Co., 1995) True story of a teacher whose son, Shin, died in the explosion while riding his new tricycle. Rich color paintings, moving text, for ages 9-12. Won Ehon Nippon Prize.

<u>Hiroshima</u>, by Laurence Yep (Scholastic, 1995) Novella about a 12-year-old girl Sachi who was injured in the bombing. For older children grades 5-8.

Films and Videos

<u>After the Cloud Lifted: Hiroshima's Stories of Recovery</u> (35 min./USA / 1996/VHS). Individual stories of some of the survivors and how they began the process of healing. An ALA Selected Film For Young Adults.

<u>Atomic Café</u> (92 min./USA/1981/VHS). Through archival footage, this film captures the dawn of the nuclear age and explores the fear factor in U.S. air raid drills and propaganda. An ironic reflection of the past and present.

<u>The Day After Trinity: J. Robert Oppenheimer and the Atomic Bomb</u> (89 min./USA/1979/DVD). The story of the Manhattan Project and the scientists who created the atomic

bomb. Nominated for an Academy Award.

The Face of Jizo (100 min. Japan/2004). Directed by Kazuo Kuroki, an adaptation of a play by Hisashi Inoue. Poignant yet humorous story of a Hiroshima survivor who rediscovers the will to live through her ghost father.

Hiroshima Nagasaki 1945 (18 min./USA/1970/VHS). Edited by noted film historian Eric Barnouw, this short silent film shows U.S. military footage taken immediately after the bombings and classified secret for 25 years.

The Last Atomic Bomb (92 min./USA/2006/VHS or DVD). produced by Robert Richter and Kathleen Sullivan. Nuclear proliferation is seen through the life of a Nagasaki survivor and several college students today.

Nagasaki Journey (83 min./USA/1983). Produced by Emmy Award-winning filmmakers, the film tells the stories of two Japanese survivors and a U.S. Marine who was one of the first US troops to occupy the city after the war.

Original Child Bomb (57 min./USA/2004/DVD). Rare color footage of Hiroshima and Nagasaki filmed by US military and Japanese camera crews.

White Light/Black Rain (85 min./USA/2007/DVD). HBO documentary includes interviews with 14 survivors including Mr. Taniguchi and Mrs. Nagano, plus four Americans involved in the bombings.

Rhapsody in August (98 min./Japan/1991/DVD). The final film released in the U.S. by

> "The atomic bomb survivors desire that they be the final victims of nuclear weapons. May our young people inherit this desire for peace, and ... take action, and pass on this spirit to the future."
>
> — Mayor Iccho Itoh of Nagasaki

Akira Kurosawa looks at the bombing of Nagasaki after more than 40 years, through the eyes of a woman who survived and her grandchildren.

Questions for Discussion and Reflection

The stories in this book can provoke much thought and conversation at home, in the classroom, and in religious and community settings. For too long, the discussion of nuclear weapons has been left to specialists. Many basic questions surrounding nuclear weapons and war are questions of human values and choices that each of us must ponder. These sample questions are not meant to be exhaustive, but simply a place to start.

1. Do you, your parents, or grandparents remember the bombings of Hiroshima or Nagasaki? What were your or their feelings at the time? Try to recall specific conversations or reactions. Have your or their views changed since then?

2. How might the bombings of Hiroshima and Nagasaki have looked to the Japanese people at the time? How might their views have changed, and why?

3. Some of the scientists who helped create the bombs petitioned President

Truman not to use them. What values might lead someone to work on nuclear weapons and then recommend that they not be used?

4. Every U.S. President since 1945 has expressed concern about nuclear weapons. Yet each has added more weapons of greater sophistication and destructive power to the U.S. arsenal. What political or psychological forces can lead to such contradictions?

5. How do the experiences of Hiroshima and Nagasaki shed light on the effectiveness of emergency planning in the event of a nuclear war?

6. What views do your government representatives favor as ways to prevent the dangers of nuclear weapons? Do you agree with them?

7. Has terrorism changed your opinions about nuclear weapons? How and why?

Projects for Teachers

1. Have your students each pick one person in this book and write a letter, draw an illustration, or write a poem for them.

2. Learn to fold origami paper cranes and read the story of Sadako together.

3. Have older students choose an issue in current events that involves nuclear

What views do your government representatives favor as ways to prevent the dangers of nuclear weapons? Do you agree with them?

137

weapons, and write letters to their government representatives.

4. Have older students research and play the roles of nuclear scientists who created the atomic bomb, some of whom opposed and some favored its use.

Internet Resources

The Internet offers a vast array of web sites that contain important historical and authoritative material about the bombings of Hiroshima and Nagasaki.

The **Hiroshima Peace Memorial Museum** has a comprehensive web site (http://www.pcf.city.hiroshima.jp/) in both English and Japanese. So does the **Nagasaki Atomic Bomb Museum** (http://www1.city.nagasaki.nagasaki.jp/na-bomb/museum/museume01.html). Both have links to many other useful sites.

The Nuclear Files website (http://www.nuclearfiles.org/menu/key-issues/nuclear-weapons/history/pre-cold-war/hiroshima-nagasaki/index.htm) is a good place to find primary source material relating to the bombings.

The Internet offers a vast array of web sites that contain important historical and authoritative material about the bombings of Hiroshima and Nagasaki.

What Else Can We Do?

A wide range of resources about nuclear weapons is available for concerned citizens of all political persuasions. Some groups offer student memberships, newsletters, magazines, and opportunities for action. They include:

Abolition 2000 (www.abolition2000.org)

Arms Control Association   (www.armscontrol.org)

Center for Arms Control and Non-Proliferation (nukesofhazard.blogspot.com)

Council for a Livable World   (www.clw.org)

Educators for Social Responsibility (esrinternational.org)

Federation of Atomic Scientists (www.fas.org)

Friends Committee on National Legislation (www.fcnl.org)

International Atomic Energy Association (www.iaea.org)

International Physicians for the Prevention of Nuclear War

Mayors for Peace (www.2020visioncampaign.org)

Physicians for Social Responsibility   (www.psr.org)

"To remember the past is to commit oneself to the future. To remember Hiroshima is to abhor nuclear war. To remember Hiroshima is to commit oneself to peace."

— Pope John Paul II, 1981

Acknowledgments and Thanks

Mayors Tadatoshi Akiba and the late Iccho Itoh & the Cities of Hiroshima & Nagasaki

Chugoku Shimbun Newspaper, Nagasaki Broadcasting Co., & RCC Broadcasting Co.

Hiroshima International Cultural Foundation

Hiroshima Peace Memorial Museum and Nagasaki Atomic Bomb Museum

Mr. Yasuhiko Yamamoto, Hiroshima Convention & Visitors Bureau

Faculty at Hiroshima University and Hiroshima Jogakuin University

Akira Tashiro, Hiroshi Sunairi, Nobuto Sugiura, Noriyuki Masuda, Natsuki and Michiko Okita, Tomoko Watanabe, Naoko Shigetaka, Shinji Hayashi, Koichi Okada, and many others in Hiroshima and Nagasaki

Translators: Yumiko Mikame, Hatsue Abe, Michiko Shishido, Michiko Tashiro

teach us to live

Father Jose Aguilar of the Nagai Student Center in Nagasaki

World Friendship Center & Aster Plaza in Hiroshima

Steve Leeper, Hiroshima Peace Culture Foundation

Ann Sherif, Randy Coleman, Nancy Dye, Ron DiCenzo, Shozo Kawaguchi, Paula Richman, Karen and Paul Moser of Oberlin College

Deborah Lubar, Harley Francis and the casts of *Ghosts of Hiroshima*

Tom Bethel of Acoustik Musik, Ltd.

Oberlin Shansi Memorial Foundation

The American Friends Service Committee

Great Lakes Colleges Association

Ohio Humanities Council

Wilmington College Peace Resource Center

My friends and family

And especially the *hibakusha*.

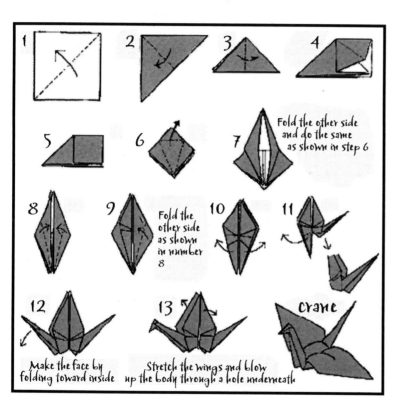

Paper crane folding instructions

143